A History of the
Chartered Institute
of Arbitrators

NIGEL WATSON

Course Information

Module 1 – Commercial Mediation Training

A History of the
Chartered Institute
of Arbitrators

NIGEL WATSON

A History of the Chartered Institute of Arbitrators

© 2015 The Chartered Institute of Arbitrators

Design and compilation © 2015 The Chartered Institute of Arbitrators and

James & James (Publishers) Limited

Produced by James & James (Publishers) Limited, a subsidiary of Third Millennium Information Limited,

2–5 Benjamin Street, London EC1M 5QL, United Kingdom

www.tmiltd.com

JAMES
X
JAMES

ISBN: 978 1 908990 24 2

British Library Cataloguing in Publication Data
A CIP catalogue record for this book is available from the British Library

Written by Nigel Watson
Edited by Hannah Bowen
Production by Debbie Wayment
Reprographics by Tag Publishing, London
Printed and bound by 1010 International Limited, China

CONTENTS

FOREWORD

For those looking for a treatise, textbook or practitioners' guide on international arbitration, this is not the book for you. This is a book, rather, for those interested in the origins and evolution of an institution which has, for the better part of its century of existence, ventured to the furthest corners of the globe as it carries out its mission to educate and promote the practice of international arbitration internationally. This is a book that captures for posterity, the aspirations and dreams of the brilliant visionaries who, collectively, have contributed to the development and internationalization of the practice of arbitration.

It is divided into four parts of equal significance. Part 1 begins with an overview of the Institute and its journey from modest beginnings to the organization that it is today – 13,500 members spread across 125 countries. Founded in 1915, the remarkable work and achievements of the Chartered Institute of Arbitrators over the last hundred years might be overlooked if we did not retain a perspective of this historical journey. From its earliest days, an international outlook was present with the first overseas foray, the formation of a branch in New South Wales, Australia, undertaken in 1927 just a dozen years after its foundation. As the Institute gradually established itself internationally, a common theme emerges: much of the success of the Institute is attributable to the courage, ambition and unbridled passion of its past leaders and members who were ardent in realizing their goal of promoting the truly international practice of arbitration. As the Institute consolidated its strength of position as a

The Patron of the Institute of Arbitrators, Sundaresh Menon, Chief Justice of the Supreme Court of Singapore.

thought leader in the field of international arbitration, it understood the importance of contributing academically to the legal jurisprudence. The Institute is now widely recognized as a learned society promoting and undertaking highly regarded academic work. It has also broadened its mission to embrace, promote and encourage a better understanding of other methods of alternative dispute resolution (ADRs) such as conciliation and mediation.

Part 2 takes the reader back in time and deeper into the history of the Institute that has been neatly separated into four crucial periods, starting with the humble beginnings of the Institute and its founders. The next two periods stretching from 1918 to 1971 are dotted with the struggles and difficulties the Institute faced in its journey towards internationalization. Nevertheless, these obstacles were overcome and, as its global footprint expanded, the Institute focused on transforming itself into a more professional organization, befitting its increasingly diverse and distinguished membership. In this fourth period, the Institute's rise to prominence was capped with the granting of a Royal Charter and the appointment of a succession of distinguished judges from the United Kingdom as Honorary Presidents.

Part 3 highlights the reformative work of the Institute. It begins with a recap of the various reforms that international arbitration has seen since the turn of the nineteenth century. The Institute had a hand in either driving or contributing to many of these. Recognizing that achieving and maintaining high professional standards of arbitrators is key to the continued success of international arbitration, the Institute has in recent times concentrated its reform efforts on improving the quality of arbitrators through structured education. The Institute's quest for improvement has not been confined to international arbitration. Since as early as 1975, the Institute saw the scope for other forms of alternative dispute resolution mechanisms to complement international arbitration, and the Institute has ventured to do for these what it has done and continues to do for international arbitration.

As the only international membership body for the profession, the Institute's work in the past hundred years has resulted in the institutionalization of systemic processes, knowledge creation and management, and the enhancement of core competencies, all of which will enable the Institute to play a pivotal role in shaping dispute resolution for the twenty-first century. Through Part 4 of the book, the Institute makes it clear that this vital role, though daunting, is one that the Institute is eager to assume. From the training of arbitrators to the formulation of best practices, to nurturing the next generation of the membership, to enhancing the visibility of the organization, and everything in between, the Institute is raring to go.

Without downplaying the achievements of the Institute in the last century, I am supremely confident that this honourable organization has all the political will, social clout and institutional expertise to serve the global community with the sort of distinction that it has come to be associated with, and accomplish even more in the next century.

It is truly my privilege and honour as the current Patron of the Institute to introduce and commend this Centenary book.

SUNDARESH MENON
Chief Justice of Singapore and Patron of
the Chartered Institute of Arbitrators

Part 1

THE 21ST-CENTURY INSTITUTE

AN INTERNATIONAL INSTITUTE

The Chartered Institute of Arbitrators has pursued the international promotion of arbitration ever since its foundation in 1915, but it is only since the 1970s that it has developed a global membership network. Today the Institute's qualifications have gained worldwide recognition: with approximately 13,000 members, this makes the Chartered Institute a unique global organization in its field.

The Chartered Institute of Arbitrators is dedicated to the promotion not only of arbitration but also of all alternative methods of resolving disputes, including mediation, conciliation and adjudication. Uniquely the Institute is the only arbitral membership body with a worldwide presence. Arbitration has always been a secondary profession, with arbitrators traditionally drawn from a wide range of other occupations, including architects, engineers and lawyers.

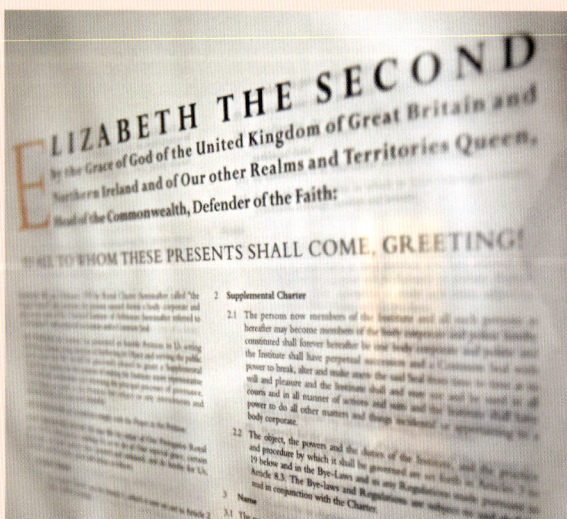

The Institute was first granted a Royal Charter in 1979.

For international practitioners, often involved in cases covering several jurisdictions, the Institute's Fellowship and Chartered Arbitrator qualifications are highly regarded. As one arbitrator put it, 'They are the only meaningful credentials recognized around the world.'

The Institute was first granted a Royal Charter in 1979. The great strength of the Institute is its international scope, invaluable in a world where the transnational nature of commerce has blurred the arbitral boundaries between common law, civil law and other jurisdictions. The Royal Charter, modified in 2005, sets out the Institute's main purpose: 'to promote and facilitate worldwide the determination of disputes by arbitration and alternative means of private dispute resolution other than resolution by the court'. Today the Institute has approximately 13,000 members spread across 125 countries, with 60 per cent outside Great Britain and Ireland.

This internationalization is a relatively recent development. When the Hong Kong branch was formed in 1972, the Institute had just 2,200 members, and by far the greatest number of them were found in England.

There had been earlier attempts to spread the gospel of arbitration beyond the shores of the United Kingdom to the far outposts of the British Empire. Applications were

made to the Institute in 1926 to form branches in India and New South Wales, and in 1927, when the Institute's entire membership was fewer than 300, a branch was started in Sydney. In the late 1920s the Federation of the Chambers of Commerce of the British Empire, striving to develop arbitration rules for acceptance in the dominions and colonies, hoped that the Institute would promote branches overseas as a way of supplying an international body of qualified arbitrators.

In fact, this would take more than 40 years to materialize. For a long time the Institute was represented overseas by just a handful of corresponding members scattered throughout the Commonwealth. Over the years a few members sought to raise the Institute's profile beyond the UK. One of the most notable was Cedric Barclay, a renowned maritime arbitrator, whose international vision was ahead of his time.

It was at Barclay's initiative that members began attending international conferences. During 1969–70, his year as President, he arranged a visit to the Third International Arbitration Conference in Venice and a joint three-day conference with French arbitrators in Le Touquet. In 1972, during Clifford Clark's year as President, 40 members attended the Fourth Conference in Moscow. Bill James, the immediate past President, gave a presentation at the Conference, noting that the Institute had members in

Presidents

1969–70: Cedric Barclay

A well-respected and well-liked international maritime arbitrator, Cedric Barclay was President of the London Maritime Arbitrators Association as well as President of the Institute, of which he became a Fellow in 1958. He was also a founding member of the International Council for Commercial Arbitration in 1972. Educated in Istanbul and Lausanne, he held degrees in mechanical engineering from London and in naval architecture from Durham. As another member, Ron Baden Hellard, later described him, Barclay was 'a powerhouse of energy, initiative, vision, language, innovation and leadership'. As an arbitrator, he was very fair, always acting as a friendly inquisitor, always seeking to understand the strengths of the weaker party's case. With his extensive international experience (he was a man who spoke at least eight languages), he was instrumental in beginning the process of broadening the Institute's horizons and raising its global profile.

Cedric Barclay (second from left).

six European countries, eight Asian countries, six countries in the Americas and ten in Africa, as well as Australia and New Zealand.

James was one of several members who made an impact at the Moscow Conference by presenting a series of papers on effective practice in arbitration. Barclay himself had emphasized the need for better communications between national arbitration associations, and urged experienced national arbitrators to spread their wings and take up international work. He was behind the first incarnation of the Institute's international committee in 1973 and continued to work hard to build up the Institute's profile worldwide. Under his guidance, the committee gained an understanding of how arbitration operated outside the UK and organized a series of lectures for members on comparative arbitration law and practice. The committee also sought unsuccessfully to persuade the UK government to ratify the 1958 New York Convention on the Recognition and Enforcement of Foreign Arbitral Awards – an indication of the low priority given at the time to international, as opposed to domestic, arbitration. Visits to international conferences continued: 25 members attended the Fifth Conference in New Delhi in 1975, and in 1980 another party went to the Bermuda conference organized with the American Arbitration Association and the Arbitrators' Institute of Canada.

In the meantime the Hong Kong branch had been formed, in February 1972. The first chairman of the new branch was Harold Miller and its first secretary Dick Tok, while the Institute's corresponding member in the territory, Ernest Low, also played a significant role. It was a prescient move, for arbitration was then used only rarely in what was still a British colony. But very soon China began to open up to international trade and there was a growing interest in oil and gas exploration. This encouraged such moves to establish Hong Kong as a regional arbitration centre, and Low could report that 'Hong Kong has suddenly woken up to international commercial arbitrations'. With 370 members, the Hong Kong branch soon afterwards began providing local education and training courses. It outstripped by a long way the number of members in nearby countries. Malaysia, for instance, had 31 members, and Singapore, 51.

In fact, Hong Kong's example was rather frowned upon by the Institute in London. General policy was to encourage 'overseas' members to promote arbitration through their own national associations where they existed rather than form new branches. But Bertie Vigrass, the Institute's energetic Secretary from 1972 to 1986, acknowledged in 1980 that 'membership of the Chartered Institute is becoming "international"', and the Institute agreed to back new branches wherever there was enough support. Senior members were also eager for expansion. As Chairman of the Institute in 1983–4, Ray Turner, a distinguished construction arbitrator, later the first Visiting Professor of Arbitration at Leeds Metropolitan University, set up a working party specifically to examine further geographical (and occupational) expansion.

The Institute has 37 branches throughout the world.

Institute members networking.

Yet only three more international branches joined Hong Kong during this period. The Republic of Ireland branch, formed in 1981, had a wide range of members, including accountants and architects, engineers and quantity surveyors, insurers and lawyers, loss adjusters and auctioneers. In Kenya, where it was hoped arbitration might help diminish the perpetual backlog of court cases, a branch was formed in 1984. A New Zealand branch proved short-lived, breaking away from the Institute after differences to form a national association in 1988.

Despite reservations about this trend, Vigrass was nevertheless an enthusiast for international arbitration and, like Barclay, he could see the potential and the scope it could give for expansion. A European Arbitration Conference was organized in London in 1980, and, three years later, with the help of a small group of senior members including Barclay, Turner and Clifford Clark (another eminent maritime arbitrator), the Institute organized its first Symposium on International Commercial Arbitration. This was stimulated by the adoption in 1976 of the United Nations Commission on International Trade Law (UNCITRAL) Model Rules, drafted at the request of developing nations seeking an arbitral counterweight to dominant Western arbitral systems. Heralding a major change in international commercial arbitration, this resolution by the UN General Assembly made it all the more urgent for the Institute to focus on its own worldwide ambitions.

One of the speakers at the Symposium was the Attorney General of Hong Kong, Michael Thomas, who observed that it was 'time for Hong Kong to move to overhaul its arbitration law in order to meet the demands of the commercial world'. Hong Kong's progress as a centre of international arbitration proved relentless. The new

legislation that took force in 1982 followed previous English legislation, but expressly respected the Chinese tradition of conciliation, widely employed in the business community – an interesting early example of the official adoption of forms of dispute resolution other than arbitration. In 1985, thanks to the work of a committee led by branch member David Hunter, Hong Kong's international arbitration centre was founded.

From the mid-1980s there was a renewed impetus towards internationalization, thanks to another generation of members with a clear vision of the Institute's international role. One was the Institute's President, Sir Michael Kerr, a distinguished judge, who reminded members in 1985 that the Institute was unique among similar bodies worldwide in having a reputation beyond its national borders. While the Institute's domestic role was important, so too was its international role, and the two should be given equal weight. Another was Ronald

Former Institute President Colin Wall (seventh from left) at an event in Melbourne.

Tony Canham (second from left), Maurice Pleasance (third from right) and guests.

Bernstein, a distinguished QC who had published a well-received *Handbook of Arbitration Practice* in 1987. At the Institute's conference in 1988, he suggested that the Institute should provide a pool of experienced arbitrators for cases where one or more of the parties was from a different country. While the Institute should lead the development of arbitration practice in Commonwealth countries, it should also learn from and contribute towards the practice of arbitration in other nation states. Pointing out that there were 300 members in 38 non-Commonwealth countries, Bernstein noted that seminars were already being organized to help arbitrators deal with cases where the parties came from jurisdictions with different legal systems. He also stressed the Institute's role as a membership organization in facilitating the delivery of education and training to international members.

The Institute's Chairmen began making visits to members distant from London. In 1989 Maurice Pleasance travelled to Malaysia to encourage members to form a new branch. His example was followed by his successor John Tackaberry, who had no doubts about the importance of international expansion. Nevertheless, this vision was still not universally shared, and it was with some difficulty that Tackaberry persuaded members to put aside a limited sum to pay for his overseas visits. He managed to stretch these funds to cover not only a whistle-stop tour of Africa, including Nigeria, Kenya, Zimbabwe and South Africa, but also a visit to Asia. He also recognized the importance of the membership in Hong Kong and it was there that the Institute held its conference in 1991.

By this time – as one of the branch's leading members, Neil Kaplan, outlined – Hong Kong had become the largest international branch, accounting for 12 per cent of the Institute's members. In 1997, as Hong Kong was handed back to China, the branch was renamed East Asia, embracing many neighbouring countries. As more members in the region joined the Institute, junior branches

Neil Kaplan, Kerry Harding and Sir Anthony Evans, annual dinner, March 2000.

called chapters were formed. This occurred for the first time in 2006 during the Presidency of Colin Wall, who himself had been chairman of the branch in 1997. In turn these chapters became full branches, including Singapore, Thailand and Malaysia. The industrial might of China, which acted as a magnet for international trade in the new millennium, also stimulated the growth of the Institute. The East Asia branch had already organized courses in construction arbitration in China on the Institute's behalf in 2001. Five years later, the East Asia branch initiated two Chinese groups – one in Beijing, the other in Shanghai. By then the East Asia branch was the largest in the Institute, with even more members than the London branch.

The dynamic growth of the branch in Hong Kong, which mirrored the dramatic rise of the Asian economies, set the trend for the Institute. By 1994 almost a third of the 7,688 members were international. It was appropriate that Neil Kaplan should chair the reincarnation of the International Committee. The Institute's Chairman that year, John Sims, travelled to Asia with Kerry Harding, the Secretary General, moving on to Australia, where, largely thanks to the initiative of Doug Jones, a long-standing member and distinguished international arbitrator, another

First Australian President Doug Jones.

Dr Nael Bunni, President 2001–2.

branch was being formed, seven decades after that first branch in New South Wales. There was already a small branch in India, focused on Mumbai, although its fortunes tended to ebb and flow. A European branch was also formed, holding meetings and providing training across the Continent, helping to foster a greater understanding among all members of arbitration and dispute resolution under civil rather than common law.

Further recognition of the important contribution made by international members came in 1999, when Kaplan became the first President resident outside Great Britain and Ireland. In 2000 he was succeeded by Nael Bunni, the first person of a nationality other than British or Irish to hold the post. In the following year, when the Institute's examinations were held in 17 locations worldwide, international membership for the first time accounted for more than half of the nearly 10,000 members.

But this expansion was accompanied by a growing feeling of separation between many branches and the Institute in London. This began to change following the appointment of Dair Farrar-Hockley as Director General in 1999. Farrar-Hockley came to the Institute after a distinguished military career, retiring from the army with the rank of major general. He wanted to break down

the perception that the London-based Institute was too focused on the UK membership and too remote from the international branches. He tackled this in several ways. First, he travelled widely to visit branches across the world, understanding the value of face-to-face contact in developing good relationships. Second, he inculcated a more internationalist approach among the Institute's London staff in their dealings with members from countries outside the UK. This was achieved through better training, and the appointment of more international staff: by the time Farrar-Hockley stepped down in 2006, the Institute's 37 staff came from 13 different nationalities. Third, he decentralized the Institute's education and training activities. There was little sense in an organization with an international membership concentrating so much provision in London. Instead, appropriately qualified trainers were found to deliver courses locally.

Positive encouragement from the Institute, recognizing the global value of arbitration and other forms of dispute resolution, led to a flurry of international branches being founded in the new millennium. Both Kaplan and Bunni in their presidential years were responsible for initiating a number of new branches. The Bermuda branch began

in Kaplan's year, at his suggestion; it was soon joined by the Bahamas branch. The Caribbean chapter, embracing all the other major islands in the region – from Barbados and Trinidad and Tobago to St Lucia and the British Virgin Islands – became a full branch in 2009. Bunni was instrumental in expanding the Institute's network in the Middle East. Branches had been started in Cairo and Bahrain in 1999. In Cairo, Bunni had persuaded the city's international arbitration centre to host the new branch. In 2003 a branch was set up in Lebanon, where prosperity was returning, and a branch covering the United Arab Emirates (UAE) was established in 2005. The UAE branch proved particularly successful and by 2015 had more than 800 members. During the first decade of the 21st century Institute branches and chapters began to multiply in other regions, including Africa, North America and Europe.

The greatest concentration of the Institute's members remains in the UK, as it has done since the Institute was founded. Yet even in the UK few branches existed until relatively recently. After the Second World War, the UK membership had expanded steadily: many new members were involved in construction arbitration, as a more prosperous economy spawned countless new

Members of the Cyprus branch, 2013.

building projects. By the early 1970s, it seemed obvious to John Corkill, Chairman of the Membership Committee, that as a membership organization the Institute had to improve links with the rising number of members outside London. At the time the only branch in the UK was the Scottish branch, formed in 1967. With a more dispersed

membership, whose only relationship with the Institute came through its journal, training courses and visits to the London office, Corkill felt it was essential to engage more members through founding more branches. The first was the West Midlands branch in 1976, followed by a spate of new branches between 1979 and 1981, including the North West, North East, East Midlands, Western Counties, Thames Valley and South East, while the Channel Islands was added in 1983. The most significant branch was the South East, both in terms of number of members and its programmed activities, until the London branch was formed in 1992.

Following the example of Maurice Pleasance and John Tackaberry, the role of the Chairman/President as a global ambassador has become well-established, evolving into an invaluable link between London and the branches. A visit from the President serves multiple purposes. First, it boosts the morale of existing branches. In 2007, for instance, Hew Dundas reported on his visit to Lebanon, 'where not only did I find a wonderful city exuding renewed hope via regeneration, but where I also saw [Institute] membership

Annual dinner, March 2002: guests include, from the left, Steve Lawrence (3), husband of Victoria Russell (4), John Tackaberry (9), Karen Gough (10), Lord Fraser (11), Lady Evans (12) and Sir Anthony Evans (12).

at its best, with a thriving, energetic, dynamically-led Branch uniquely placed to play an essential role in the rebuilding of a war-damaged country'. Second, it introduces the Institute to new territories. Dundas had also visited South America, spending time in Ecuador, Chile and Bolivia, where the Institute was hoping to develop a network of members. Third, it helps to fulfil the Institute's principal aim of promoting arbitration worldwide. During John Campbell's year as President in 2009, he challenged law societies and bar associations around the world to make greater use of arbitration and other methods of dispute resolution. When Doug Jones, President in 2011, visited Australia, he met with most State Attorneys-General, encouraging them to go ahead with proposed arbitration reforms. In the following year Jeffrey Elkinson was welcomed warmly in Dubai, where the responsible minister invited the Institute to organize arbitration courses for his civil servants. Fourth, it encourages members to form new branches or chapters. Colin Wall, for instance, President in 2006, used his role to promote the participation of younger members in the work of the Institute, resulting in the formation of the first Young Members' Groups in Hong Kong and Nigeria.

By the mid-2000s, the strongest branches were organizing impressive activity programmes. The Ireland branch, for instance, was not untypical in running its own courses and making its own appointments. The courses and lectures of the European branch were held across the continent, from Sofia and Warsaw to Heidelberg and Malta. The Young Members' Group in the East Asia branch arranged visits to arbitral bodies in Beijing and planned a Young Members' Group international conference in Hong Kong.

Today branch chairs from around the world have their own forum through an international biennial congress, and the Chartered Institute is organized internationally on a regional basis, covering Africa, the Americas, Asia, Australasia, Europe, Great Britain, Ireland, the Middle East and the Indian Subcontinent.

2

A LEARNED SOCIETY

In recent years the Institute has placed more emphasis on developing its role as a learned society. The Institute's journal, Arbitration, *has gained a respected reputation as an academic publication. The Institute has broadened its remit to embrace methods of dispute resolution other than arbitration, such as conciliation and mediation. This process has been enhanced in recent years by investment in the Institute's research department.*

One of the ways in which the Chartered Institute sought to promote arbitration around the world was, as set out in the Royal Charter, through 'the promotion and dissemination, as a learned society, of a wider knowledge of private dispute resolution by means of meetings, conferences, seminars and lectures and by the publication of relevant materials, including a journal, and other literature'.

The growing number of international members gave this aim a renewed impetus in the 1990s. The journal, *Arbitration*, began to move away from being simply an organ of communication with members. Alan Shilston, the editor from 1980 until 1999, believed it should cater for a wide range of professional interests among the Institute's 8,500 members. Of those members whose

primary professions were known, nearly a third were surveyors (2,700). Lawyers (1,590) were the second most numerous group, followed by engineers (820), architects (570), insurers (290) and accountants (140). As a letter from one member, G. M. Beresford Hartwell, observed in 1996, this was just the latest development in the journal's evolution, having sown the seeds for many years 'of what seems now to be a world-wide interest in a more radical approach to the twin principles that persons have a right to agree between themselves and to provide for their differences to be resolved in a manner of their own making'.

Under Shilston, there was an eagerness to use the journal to exchange knowledge with colleagues worldwide and to encourage the development of a global philosophy of arbitration. In Shilston's words, 'arbitration is a technique of transmitting civilization: peace without recrimination'.

Shilston's successor, Dr Michael O'Reilly, did much to transform the journal's reputation. A qualified barrister and engineer, he had been a professor of civil engineering before concentrating on arbitration. He was the Institute's legal advisor in 1993–4 and although he would initially spend only a year as editor, he would return in 2011.

His first issue in 2000 comprised contributions from five distinguished arbitrators, invited to write an award on the same hypothetical case. In that issue he wrote that he believed the journal could make an important contribution towards the role of the Institute in 'the development and maintenance of a skilled band of arbitrators who can operate at the highest levels, nationally and internationally'.

Michael O'Reilly remained a member of a strengthened editorial board when he handed over the reins to his successor, Professor Derek Roebuck. A lawyer with international experience, Roebuck, who remained editor until 2011, had a specialist interest in the history of arbitration. He set out the journal's editorial policy in the Institute's annual report for 2005: 'to serve all members equally, wherever they are and whatever their interests, and to assist the Institute to discharge its responsibility to be a learned society'. The transformation of *Arbitration* into a journal of global scope, aiming to be both academic and practical, with distinguished contributors, was reflected in the change of its subtitle in 2007 from *The Journal of the Chartered Institute of Arbitrators* to *The International Journal of Arbitration, Mediation and Dispute Management.*

Conferences were still a major part of the Institute's drive to disseminate information on arbitration and other methods of dispute resolution, such as the Alternative Dispute Resolution (ADR) conference organized by the Malaysian branch in 2008, when the keynote address was given by the country's prime minister, or the Asia-Pacific Conference held in Sydney in 2011. By then the Institute was also investing in its own research department. This has made a growing contribution in numerous and diverse areas of arbitration and ADR, including the preparation of various publications. Many of these have been translated into several languages, recognizing the Institute's international readership.

Left, above and top right: conferences disseminate the Institute's expertise across the world.

3

PROGRESS IN GOVERNANCE

The Institute's success in recruiting more members worldwide stimulated progress in its aspiration to become an international organization. In particular, this resulted in reform of the Institute's governance to reflect this wider membership.

The growth in membership would transform the way the Institute was governed. By the late 1980s the Council, the main decision-making body, had changed little since the Institute's foundation. Although a few members had international experience, most of them were drawn from a background in domestic construction arbitration. It was over-large, inward-looking and resistant to change. In 1985 the Institute's President, Sir Michael Kerr, suggested that the time had come to alter the composition of Council to take into account the international membership. In 1988 fellow members Ronald Bernstein and Kenneth Severn echoed Kerr's views, pointing out that the Institute's decision-makers reflected neither the growth in international members nor the fact that most arbitrations occurred not in construction but in commodities, shipping and consumer services. Of the Council's 25 members, 18 came from construction backgrounds.

The Institute was becoming a much bigger body. In 1989 it had 6,782 members. Two-thirds were still based in the UK but most were outside London. A larger overall membership, and an ambition to continue expanding, made it imperative that the Institute's management and decision-making become more professional and efficient. A series of incremental changes were adopted during the 1990s. First, a regional structure was introduced. This was applied initially within the UK with regional representatives elected to the Council. The first region outside the UK was Europe, following the creation of the successful Europe branch. Second, branches were given greater autonomy. Third, to give more recognition to international members, two new posts of Vice-President (Overseas) were created in 1994 and 1996, the first post filled initially by Neil Kaplan, and international members were elected to the Council for the first time. Fourth, to make decision-making

Ken Severn and Bea Turner.

The Institute's premises on Bloomsbury Sqaure.

more efficient, a ten-strong Executive Board was formed, accountable to Council. The post of Secretary was renamed Secretary General, and later Director General. In 1999 the position of President, previously an honorary position often occupied by distinguished members of the judiciary, became an elected role, initially running in tandem with a new honorary presidency.

It was clear to the new Director General, Dair Farrar-Hockley, however, that these changes were insufficient. He understood at once that the Institute's aspirations to become an international organization were not best served by its existing form of governance. The Council was still too large, met too infrequently, and its members remained unrepresentative of the membership as a whole. He was invited to carry out a strategic review of the Institute. As part of this review, he travelled extensively overseas to elicit the views of international members.

Farrar-Hockley was also faced with other challenges. At the time the Institute was housed in unsuitable offices at a location (Angel Gate) distant from the centre of London. One of the Institute's perpetual disadvantages as a body with a limited membership was that it never had the resources to acquire a permanent home. Since its foundation it had moved from one leased property to another. But the work of Bertie Vigrass, Secretary during the 1970s and 1980s, in reviving the Institute, and his successor, Kerry Harding, in carefully husbanding the organization's finances, had resulted for the first time in significant financial reserves. Farrar-Hockley, supported by Malcolm McMullan, the recently appointed director of finance, and backed by the members, embarked on a search for freehold premises close to the City and in 2001 the Institute took ownership of a handsome Georgian building at 12, Bloomsbury Square.

Farrar-Hockley was supported by successive Chairmen of the Executive Board in devising this new strategy. John Campbell, who became Chairman in 2003, was particularly helpful, keenly aware that international members needed a greater say in the running of the Institute. Following consultation, the eventual strategy, entitled Agenda for Change, had three principal priorities. First, international promotion of the idea that private dispute resolution was a more flexible, less expensive and less time-consuming option than litigation. Second, offering education and training to those seeking to qualify as practitioners and others with an interest in the subject. Third, disseminating knowledge and information on private dispute resolution through the Institute's role as a learned society. The Institute would also examine and assess candidates seeking its qualifications, and monitor, supervise and, if necessary, discipline members in the course of their work.

The governance changes proposed the replacement of the Council with a fully elected Board of Trustees, numbering 12 members, half of whom represented regions

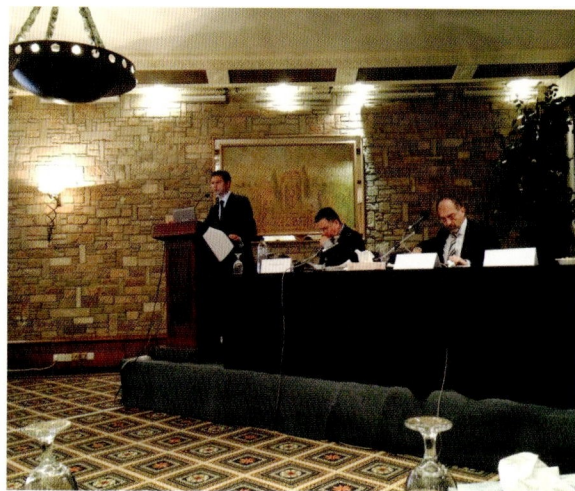

Event at the Cyprus branch, 2013.

Lord Bingham addresses the Institute.

of the world outside the UK (today a majority are from international branches). At the same time the Executive Board changed its name to the Board of Management, whose members were appointed by the Board of Trustees. Lastly, to avoid confusion, the honorary presidency would be replaced by the honorary position of Patron. These changes, together with a proposal to create the status of Chartered Arbitrator, were fundamental enough to warrant an application to revise the Royal Charter. This proved to be a complex process; it was, John Campbell recalled, 'harder making changes to the Charter than organizing a G20 summit'. The revised Royal Charter was signed and sealed on 28 February 2005, on which day the first meeting of the new Board of Trustees took place, followed the next day by the first Congress. Appropriately, given the Institute's expanding horizons, the location was Cyprus.

These changes won huge support from the Institute's members. A small group of them had shouldered most of the responsibility for driving through change, with the support of the Director General, Dair Farrar-Hockley. These included James Leckie and Brian Eggleston, successively Presidents of the Institute in 2003–4 and 2004–5, John Campbell, Chairman of the Institute's Executive Board, and Mark Entwistle.

It was Farrar-Hockley's successor as Director General, Michael Forbes Smith, who successfully implemented the changes enshrined in the new Royal Charter. Appointed in 2006, he came to the Institute after a distinguished career in the diplomatic service. The reformed system of governance worked well, but ran into difficulties with a new generation of Trustees, who found it hard to divorce their strategic role from the day-to-day management role of the Board of Management. The resulting breakdown in relationships proved to be one of the rockier patches in the Institute's recent history, but it was resolved through a special governance tribunal. Its report, delivered in 2011, recommending that post-holders should adhere to the responsibilities of already clearly defined roles, underlined the progress the Institute had already made in creating a more transparent system of governance, and allowed it to look outwards once more with confidence. While work remains to be done to continue this process, Jeffrey Elkinson was not alone in believing that 'it was a fantastic outcome and we've got a lot stronger as a result'.

Institute President Karen Gough with members, 2001–2.

Part 2

THE INSTITUTE'S PIONEERS

Arthur Marriott
Room

4

THE INSTITUTE BEGINS

Arbitration is age-old but the antecedents of English arbitration law date from the mid-nineteenth century. Weaknesses in the law and the poor portrayal of arbitrators led a group of experienced practitioners to establish the Institute for the purposes of promoting arbitration and raising the reputation of arbitrators.

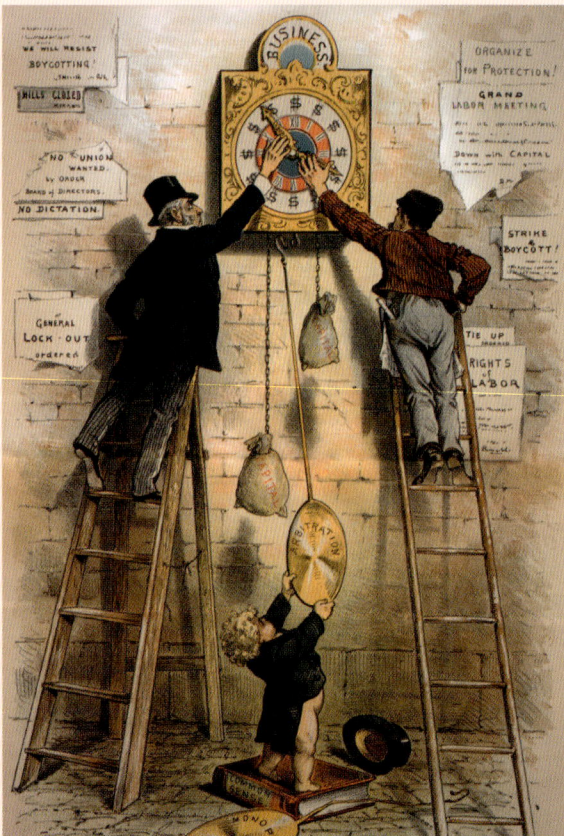

In this 1886 cartoon from Puck, arbitration is represented by the pendulum which regulates the clock of business – the two men are admonished not to meddle with the hands.

Arbitration, mediation and conciliation were first applied to international trade and commerce long ago. They were defined succinctly in 1986 by John Phillips, a distinguished member of the Institute, in an article in *Arbitration*. Arbitration arises from a dispute between parties, where they agree to refer the matter to an arbitrator for a decision they accept as legally binding. Conciliation and mediation, neither of which are legally binding, both involve a third party bringing together the parties in dispute to help them to reconcile their differences; a mediator would also suggest the terms upon which a resolution might be achieved.

There is evidence that arbitration and mediation were used by Assyrian merchants and by Mesopotamians involved in family disputes. According to Aristotle, the Greeks had two types of arbitrator, one public and appointed by lot, the other private and chosen by the parties concerned in preference to seeking redress in the courts. In both cases judgement was based on equity rather than strict legal principles. The same principle was adopted for arbitration by the Romans. In the medieval period, with merchants trading across Europe, arbitration offered a simple, speedy and confidential solution to their disputes, a principle upheld by the Court of Star Chamber in England in 1478.

As Britain's colonies became established, creating a great trading network, the influence of English arbitration began to spread around the widening world. In 1694 arbitration was anonymously defined as 'an Award, Determination or Judgement made, given between persons in Controversie, by the Arbitrators or Umpires, there being such person or persons as are thereunder elected, by the parties controverting, for the ending and Pacifying the said Controversie or Compromise of the said Parties, and agreeable to Reason and good conscience'.

By 1698, and the enactment of a statute 'for determining differences by arbitration', there were three routes to arbitration. First, there was the traditional method at common law without the involvement of the court, with the parties agreeing on an arbitrator to determine the issues privately; either party was free to reject unilaterally

Ancient Arbitration

(From a miscellany of disputes, Derek Roebuck, Oxford, 2000)

'For Confucians, the aim was to protect the equilibrium by the avoidance of disputes. They believed it was achievable and there were myths of how it had been achieved. One described how, during the Zhou dynasty (1046–256 BC), when Zhou Wen Wang governed in Xi Zhou, there were no disputes, and not a single crime for forty years. Zhou was such an able mediator that people from outside the kingdom flocked to Xi Zhou to seek his assistance. But, so the story goes, once they got there and saw how tranquil it was, they were so ashamed that they resolved their differences themselves.'

the authority of the arbitrator, although this made the party liable to an action for breach of contract. Second, the court could refer a pending case for arbitration, although the arbitrator was liable for misconduct. Third, there was the 1698 Act, designed to foster trade, make arbitral awards more effective, and bring certainty to the whole process. In particular, it allowed the parties to bring a case for contempt in the event of the non-performance of an arbitral award, and also allowed the courts to set aside an award in certain circumstances.

Judicial intervention, fostered by a dislike of arbitration among many English judges, who regarded it as an intrusion upon their own responsibilities, was already an established part of the process, and would remain so until the late twentieth century. During the eighteenth century it also became common for the parties to ask the court to set aside an arbitral award on errors in law or fact. In the early nineteenth century the courts took it upon themselves to

Scott v Avery, 1856

Avery ran a Protecting & Indemnity Club in Newcastle in the 1850s, the Club Rules insisting that any plaintiff must first obtain an arbitral award in his favour before taking legal action against the Club. Scott, a shipowner, was dissatisfied with the sum offered to settle his claim and took his case to court. It reached the House of Lords, the highest court in the land, which confirmed the ruling of the Court of Appeal that Scott should indeed have first obtained an arbitral award. This decision had a pronounced influence on the use of arbitration clauses in insurance contracts.

interfere with an arbitral award where the reasoning for the arbitrator's conclusions was inadequate. This was resented by arbitrators, who began to set down their awards in writing, although these were confidential. They also began to present cases on a point of law for the opinion of the

Cartoon from *Puck*, *c.*1889, depicting arbitration as the solution to disputes between employers and workers.

Portrait of J. R. W. Alexander at the Institute's Bloomsbury Square premises.

Presidents

1915–18: Rowland Allanson-Winn, 5th Baron Headley

A successful civil engineer, Lord Headley worked in Kashmir before returning to Dublin to found his own consultancy. He also served as President of the Society of Engineers in 1921. Aged 60 when he became the Institute's President, he was better known for his conversion to Islam in 1913; ten years later he became the first Englishman to openly undertake the pilgrimage to Mecca. He was offered the throne of Albania three times and three times turned it down.

courts, which would later be enshrined as the 'Special Case' procedure in the Common Law Procedure Act of 1854. The Act also obliged the arbitrator to issue a valid award.

The industrialization of the UK, and the great increase in trade that went with it, led to the rapid growth of arbitration and the passing of the first Arbitration Act in 1889. The Act was widely welcomed, especially in helping to achieve amicable resolutions, free from the costs and delays of the law. To be effective then, as now, arbitration depended upon skilled and experienced professional arbitrators, but it soon became apparent that the necessary knowledge, expertise and character was too often lacking in too many of them.

It was to solve this problem and to enhance the reputation of arbitrators and arbitration that the Institute of Arbitrators was formed in London on 1 March 1915. The notion came from H. C. Emery, a London solicitor who was a persistent advocate of arbitration in place of litigation wherever possible. In late 1914 he conceived the idea of

'banding together the members of those professions engaged in Arbitration', as the Institute's journal would later record.

Emery and his fellow founders, F. Malcolm Burr, an architect, I. W. Bullen, an accountant, A. Powells, a surveyor, and A. Stevens, another solicitor, were ambitious for the new organization, whose aim was 'to raise the status of Arbitrator to the dignity of a distinct and recognized position as one of learned professions'. The original objects

stressed the need to support and protect the character, status and interests of the arbitral profession. This would be achieved by testing through examination the qualifications of candidates for membership, by encouraging the practice of settling disputes by resolution, and by promoting the study of the law and practice relating to arbitration and, where necessary, supporting its reform. There was also provision to set up branches for members not only in the United Kingdom but also in Britain's colonies and dominions, and to pursue when appropriate the grant of a Royal Charter in furthering the Institute's aim. The Institute's governing body, the Council, not only reflected the diverse occupations of professional arbitrators, but also indicated the strong backing of several primary professions for the new initiative. Council members included the President and Vice-President of the Society of Architects, the President of the Society of Engineers, the President of the London Association of Accountants, two Past Presidents of the Quantity Surveyors' Association, a Past President of the Institute of Municipal Engineers and a Past

Launch of the Members' Room at 12 Bloomsbury Square, dedicated to Arthur Marriott QC, 2014.

Winchester House, Old Broad Street, home to the Institute from 1920.

Chairman of the Royal Sanitary Institute.

Emery himself became the Institute's first Secretary, but only on a part-time basis, as were all his successors until 1972. The Institute's first small office was in the heart of the City of London at 32, Old Jewry, moving in 1920 to Winchester House in Old Broad Street. By November 1915 the first issue of the Institute's journal had appeared, although it ceased publication because of the war from May 1916 until October 1920. Emery remained Secretary until his death in 1924.

The Institute's first President was Rowland Allanson-Winn, 5th Baron Headley, who served until 1918. His successor, Professor Henry Adams, was a more conventional figure. Another engineer, he was professor of engineering at the City of London College and had also served on the London Court of Arbitration, founded in 1892. Lord Headley and Adams were part of a long line of presidents who would be drawn from engineering and construction, the principal arena for arbitration in the UK at the time and for many years to come.

THE INSTITUTE 1918–39

As a new organization representing a secondary profession, the Institute found it hard to build up its membership. But its aspiration to promote arbitration around the world struck a chord. In reaction to the Great War, this was an era of internationalism, when arbitration was seen as a way of solving international political disputes. The first steps were also being taken to harmonize arbitration worldwide. The Institute was able to attract prominent people as members and honorary members, and took a leading role in the reform of English arbitration as well as a deepening interest in international commercial arbitration.

Annual dinners were established in 1928 and remained a tradition of the Institute.

Founded in the middle of a war, and finding its way during a time of post-war economic turbulence, the Institute found recruiting members a difficult task. Partly this was because, as the President, Edwin Sadgrove, put it in 1923, the Institute was choosy in who was admitted, although he emphasized that the Institute did not insist on absolute excellence, since members were offered opportunities through further training to enhance their skills. New membership classes (Retired Members and Subscribers) were created with less onerous conditions for admission, and there were attempts to recruit more members from outside construction, but neither of these initiatives was successful and in 1939 the Institute had just 350 members.

With so few members, there was never much cash in the coffers (the bank account contained just £240 in 1925). The position of Secretary could only be part-time, there were no full-time staff, and the Institute, which became a company limited by guarantee in 1925, never had a permanent home, renting a succession of small offices from sympathetic organizations. In 1929, for instance, when R. W. L. Clench and C. B. Hewitt took over from C. McArthur Butler as Joint Secretaries, their own offices just off The

Strand hosted the Institute, but meetings and lectures took place at the Embankment headquarters of the Incorporated Society of Accountants and Auditors. It was inevitable that most events were held in London, but this caused some resentment among members more distant from the capital (a tension that would be magnified much later as the number of international members rose). The Institute's small size also prevented any progress in achieving a Royal Charter, one of the Institute's objects and an aim pursued intermittently throughout the interwar period.

Even so, the Institute was already recruiting some members from outside the United Kingdom. They came mainly from the colonies and dominions, and most were expatriates. In 1927 the first branch was formed in New South Wales while in 1930–4 members from Sydney and Nairobi, Bombay and Alexandria, Singapore and Pretoria were among those elected Fellows. Occasionally the Institute admitted members from outside the boundaries of the British Empire. Selim K. Malouff from Beirut was elected a Fellow in 1930 and Leonard Adams, based in Mexico City, in 1934. Although there was some exaggeration in the words of the guest speaker at the annual dinner in 1934, his sentiments were apposite: 'Nothing but good can come of an Institute now worldwide in its membership, and particularly renowned throughout the Empire, which deals with the instruction of those who are to decide the cases of others, as something worthy of study, of application and of serious pursuit.'

There were very few women; the first female member was a barrister, Miss D. Scott Stokes, in 1931. The approach of the Institute to female members was summed up in the remarks made by the President in 1937: 'We allow ladies to come in, if sufficiently qualified'.

The Presidents following Lord Headley and Henry Adams were often architects and engineers. Most of them were well versed in construction arbitration, such as Horace Boot, a consulting engineer who was President in 1923–4. One of several interwar Presidents who were also experienced expert witnesses, Boot specialized in

'The Conciliator' – caricature of George Askwith by Wallace Hester, *Vanity Fair*, 25 October 1911.

important engineering cases. His successor, Sir Charles Ruthen (1924–5), had been Director-General of Housing, and was followed by H. B. Chaplin Baldwin (1926–8), who was unusual in being a chartered accountant. A badge of office was commissioned in 1927, designed and made by one of the country's leading silversmiths, Omar Ramsden.

The Institute's most distinguished President between the two world wars was Lord Askwith, who served between 1933 and his death in 1942. Although he had been an honorary member since 1924, Askwith's willingness to take up the office was something of a coup for the Institute.

Presidents

1933–42: George Askwith, Baron Askwith

Askwith was the outstanding industrial arbitrator and conciliator of his age. A barrister by profession, he was introduced to arbitration work in 1896, and three years later was involved in the boundary arbitration involving British Guiana and Venezuela. He was deeply involved in seeking settlements to the industrial disputes that broke out in the UK during 1911–12, for which he was knighted. His peerage came after less successful wartime service. As an arbitrator, he was patient and inscrutable, indefatigable in seeking out common ground on which to build a consensus, and happy for others to take the credit for any settlement. He was an influential President, raising the Institute's profile during the reform of English arbitration law at a time when membership was flagging.

His experience as an arbitrator touched on international boundary disputes but came predominantly from his involvement in resolving the major strikes that had unsettled the UK in the years before the First World War. This wider vision of arbitration, the belief that it could be fruitfully applied on an international scale, was not new, for there have been instances throughout history of arbitration being used to resolve disputes between states. But it was a belief held with particularly deep conviction after the horrors of the First World War, resulting in the founding of the League of Nations. While domestic construction disputes may have been the main arbitral concern of most of the Institute's members, the pages of the journal show members also took an interest in the international potential of arbitration. At the Institute's first annual dinner in 1928 the guest of honour was Viscount Cecil, a strong advocate of disarmament and supporter of the League of Nations, who subsequently became one of the Institute's honorary members. He spoke passionately about the potential of arbitration to resolve international disputes and

complimented the Institute for its promotional work.

Other honorary members included Sir Robert Horne, one-time Chancellor of the Exchequer, and Sir Josiah Stamp, the leading economist of his generation. This was all part of the efforts of a small organization representing a largely unrecognized secondary profession to achieve a higher profile. It was not easy. The Institute relied for its momentum on a handful of committed members. Audiences for lectures and mock arbitrations were often made up of members from other bodies. Few activities were organized for members outside London, who understandably took little active interest. In any case resources were very limited.

Punch cartoon following the 1899 arbitration in which George Askwith had participated: Prime Minister Lord Salisbury makes off with the disputed territory awarded to Britain.

Distinguished honorary members Sir Robert Horne and Sir Josiah Stamp.

Yet the Institute never lost sight of its objective for the wider promotion of arbitration. In December 1931, for instance, *The Arbitrator* recorded that, 'The Institute has been brought into close touch with many Institutions and Societies, to whom arbitration is important and to whom we can be of assistance. Especially we are co-operating with men and Societies of other nationalities. Many cases have been before the Institute and we have nominated arbitrators to act and also have supplied the names of qualified arbitrators to other bodies for appointment. The business man is taking more kindly to arbitration as a method of settlement of disputes'. In the early 1930s the Institute's confidence was also boosted when, under the presidency of Lord Askwith, it played the major part in securing the passage of the Arbitration Act, 1934, the first new arbitration legislation in nearly half a century.

The Institute began appointing arbitrators from within its own ranks during the 1920s. Regulations for the Appointment of Arbitrators were issued in 1925, based on the rules adopted by the London Court of Arbitration and the Society of Architects; and an Arbitration Committee was established, which compiled lists of appropriately qualified members willing to act as arbitrators. The

arbitrations were administered by the Secretary in his role as Registrar.

There was renewed energy in the Institute's activities as the 1930s drew to a close. Practice arbitrations, discussions at regular luncheon meetings, examinations covering the law of contracts, the law of arbitration, procedure and evidence, and cooperation with another appointing body, the London Court of Arbitration, all formed part of these activities, although the annual lecture series had been abandoned and there was little reference to any events occurring outside London. Collaboration was growing with other bodies, notably the London Court of Arbitration in the UK and the American Arbitration Association (AAA) overseas. Several textbooks had been published and an Arbitration Information Service had been started. The Institute's own model rules were increasingly used to conduct arbitrations. More to the point, the quality of arbitrators had improved enormously since the bad old days of the early 1900s, and the courts had become much more supportive, willing to stay proceedings and enforce a submission to arbitration, and reluctant to set aside awards. In these improvements the Institute had certainly played its part.

THE INSTITUTE 1939–71

Efforts to keep the Institute's international vision alive foundered after the war and the organization, lacking ambition, went into decline. Under a new Secretary, its revival began in the early 1960s, with the formation of the very first branch, an expansion in membership, and a renewed determination to promote the benefits of arbitration more widely.

With the outbreak of war, all fixtures for the Institute's 1939–40 session, other than examinations, were cancelled. An American arbitrator penned for the AAA's journal his recollections of attending the Institute's Annual General Meeting in London in 1941 during the height of the Blitz:

Amidst the crash of bombs, the roar of anti-aircraft guns and the falling of buildings, this pillar of freedom stands out, indicating that in the turmoil of battle the spirit of arbitration is not yet dead. It is little more than that, for in London – once the

The Bretton Woods conference of 1944 helped to usher in an internationalist spirit which fostered the use of arbitration to resolve disputes.

Beleaguered but defiant: St Paul's Cathedral, London, surrounded by the destruction caused by the Blitz, at a time the AAA's journal hailed the Institute's activities as a 'pillar of freedom'.

great center of arbitration for the trade routes of the world – the voice of arbitration no longer speaks with authority to the world.

The author contended that in relation to arbitration, given these circumstances, 'never has its survival depended so much upon America, for it is here that both its spirit and practice must find a stronghold'.

In fact wartime favoured arbitration over litigation for the settlement of disputes in the UK, and the Institute was cited more often as the appointing body when arbitration clauses were inserted into contracts. Even so, there was still great ignorance about arbitration, which the Institute was determined to do something about once peace returned.

An editorial in what was now renamed *Arbitration* expressed the hope in 1942 that 'If the happy state were reached where arbitration was considered to be the normal outlet for international troubles, this would in itself lead to Arbitration dominating not only international but national disputes and disputes between individuals'.

This internationalist spirit prevailed once again at the end of the war with the Bretton Woods agreement in 1944 and the creation of the United Nations in 1945. The Institute's new President, Sir Lynden Macassey, encouraged this spirit in the Institute, repeatedly raising the topic of international commercial arbitration during his five years in office. But despite his evangelism, there seems to have been little enthusiasm among members. Macassey stepped

Presidents

1945–50: Sir Lynden Macassey

Macassey, born in Northern Ireland, trained as an engineer before becoming a barrister and taking silk in 1912 at the age of 36. This combination led to his appointment as a Board of Trade arbitrator during the First World War, when his good work was overshadowed by his controversial role in the deportation from Glasgow of the leader of the Clyde Workers' Committee and four of his colleagues. After the war he became one of the British government's labour assessors at the International Court of Justice at The Hague.

The International Court of Justice, The Hague.

down in 1950 without having rekindled the Institute's pre-war internationalism. With his departure, the Institute abandoned the practice of appointing men eminent in their field as Presidents. The excuse was that such appointees could never find the time to do justice to the role, yet Macassey's presence is evident from the pages of the Institute journal. The practice was not revived until the appointment of Lord Diplock in 1977.

This seems to have been symptomatic of the Institute's lack of ambition in the 1940s and 1950s. It is difficult to establish why the Institute's international vision vanished. The UK endured a decade of austerity after 1945. The last building controls disappeared only in 1954 and the depressed level of construction may have had an impact on the number of arbitrations. It was also a postcolonial age, as colonies became independent and dominions loosened their ties with the mother country, perhaps discouraging Institute members from looking outwards. There certainly appears to have been a more parochial feel about the Institute. Editorials in the journal were critical. In the early 1950s these lamented the lack of leadership shown by the Institute in the field of arbitration. For Ray Turner, who joined from the provinces as a member in 1953, 'the Institute seemed almost a London club'. The Institute, it was said, had become almost unknown, and few if any contracts now stipulated the Institute as a nominating body for the appointment of arbitrators. Numbers were growing but only slowly, reaching just over 500 by the mid-1950s, and there was unhappiness that it was unrepresentative of all those professions likely to practise as arbitrators. Lawyers, in particular, were few and far between, although this was attributed to the continuing antipathy of the legal profession towards arbitration. (This was highlighted in 1955 when the Bar Council banned practising barristers from acting as counsel in the Institute's mock arbitrations on the grounds that it constituted advertising.) Even so, noted one editorial in 1953, 'until, in fact, it is truly representative, none of the other aims of the Institute will be achieved ... it should never be forgotten that arbitration proceedings are not limited to the determination of building disputes. The scope for extending the Institute's influence is immense, and should be firmly grasped'. Firmly grasped it was not. All these weaknesses were still evident to Alan Daly when he became President in 1955. His presidential address was blunt: the Institute was falling behind other more recently established professional bodies. It was, he said, in danger of becoming 'moribund'.

The pattern of activities (London lunches, London lectures, London practice arbitrations, the annual dinner) remained unchanged, as did the format of the journal. The membership had been static for some time and there was a need to recruit more widely, particularly if there was to be any possibility of forming branches outside London and employing more staff to support the Secretary. The state of the Institute was summed up when Daly asked, only half in jest, that 'my badge of office be cleaned and a new piece of ribbon put on so that when I go out representing you I will at least look clean and tidy'.

The Institute was still recruiting members from areas of imperial influence, from Baghdad and Hong Kong, Kampala and Bulawayo, Melbourne and Colombo, Wellington and Johannesburg. In the recently formed Federation of Rhodesia and Nyasaland (later to become Zambia, Malawi and Zimbabwe), expatriate Britons were seeking to set up their own arbitration panel made up of Institute members as a way of raising standards in a region where many awards were being set aside because of poorly trained and inexperienced arbitrators. They were helped by a visit from Daly, as the journal noted in 1956: 'Slowly the Institute has built solid foundations here and with the very recent visit of our Immediate Past President, Mr Alan Daly, who had been able to examine our problems and assess our requirements on the post, the erection of a solid and practical structure is now assured'. This was probably the first time anyone as senior as Daly had visited Institute members overseas.

Salisbury (later renamed Harare), capital of the Federation of Rhodesia and Nyasaland, around the time Alan Daly made his visit to Institute members there.

Social function during Margaret Rutherford's presidency, 1992–3.

Over the next few years the membership of Council was widened, with the addition of co-opted members, and by 1959 it comprised representatives from architecture, surveying, quantity surveying, building, the law, civil engineering, insurance, shipbroking and the building societies. Overall membership, however, was growing only slowly, and in 1960 Council took the extraordinary view that it was no longer viable to set up branches either in the UK or overseas, believing that the specialist nature of arbitration made such expansion impossible.

Robert Morgan, the Institute's one-time legal advisor, in a later article surveying the Institute's history, characterized this period as one of 'a semi-permanent state of collective soul-searching'. When Ronald Ward, a successful architect

whose practice designed London's Millbank Tower, became President in 1959, the Institute, the journal later recorded, 'was at a low ebb and meeting problems on all sides'. Publishing the journal itself had become one of those problems, and Ward would write large parts of it himself. Leslie Alexander, later President of the Institute in 1973–4, recalled how little known the Institute was when he joined in the early 1960s. Most active members were based in and around the capital, administration was simple and Council meetings short.

But there was a perceptible change in this ineffectual attitude from the early 1960s. Partly this was because the UK economy was prospering, Britain was in the middle of its largest ever house-building programme and demand was growing for knowledgeable and experienced arbitrators. But it also had something to do with the retirement of long-serving Secretary C. B. Hewitt in 1962 after nearly 33 years and the appointment of a new Secretary, David Reid. Although his post remained part-time, Reid's energy and enthusiasm breathed new life into the moribund organization. Things that had been done as a matter of course before the war and been largely neglected since were revived.

The Institute once again began making connections, organizing a series of private lunches with leading members of other professional bodies and government departments. Members were asked to advise the newly formed Consumer Council on arbitration and the Board of Trade on commercial arbitration in Asia. The work of the Arbitration Committee was revived, beginning in 1964 with a round-table meeting of parties interested in reforming English arbitration law, including representatives from the Bar Council, the Law Society, the Royal Institution of British Architects, the Institution of Civil Engineers and the Association of British Chambers of Commerce.

The Institute added about 100 new members every year during the 1960s and in 1965 moved into new leased premises, with a council chamber and court room, at 16, Park Crescent, London, the home of the Chartered Institute of Secretaries. By 1970, with 1,876 members, membership had more than trebled in a decade. With more members outside London, the Institute's very first branch had been formed in 1967. The idea for a Scottish branch emerged from a discussion between a group of Scottish members, led by Michael Weir, during an arbitration seminar held in the George Hotel, Edinburgh, in May 1967. Yet, as we have seen, it would be nearly a decade before the second branch followed in England.

There were also tentative signs of a renewed internationalism. The journal, which often seems to have acted as the conscience of the Institute under its various editors, urged members to be more outward-looking, given that arbitration was practised worldwide, and that the

Leslie Alexander, who joined the Institute in the 1960s.

organization still remained unknown in many parts of the world, such as Asia. In 1970, to establish links with Japan, the Institute elected as a Fellow Yasuzo Ichii, the President of the Japan Shipping Exchange. This was the same year in which Cedric Barclay became President, giving a great boost to the Institute's international vision.

Bill James, Barclay's successor as President, was also more far-sighted than most. He understood that an organization with a growing membership had much more potential. His vision encompassed developing links with consumer bodies interested in devising their own consumer arbitration schemes, as well as the promotion of arbitration on the widest scale, beyond the confines of construction, which still dominated English domestic arbitration. In time many of his aspirations would be achieved but any initial progress depended on strengthening the infrastructure of the Institute.

7

THE INSTITUTE 1971–99

With a full-time Secretary for the first time, the Institute began to develop into a more professional organization. The rapid rise in members, and the formation of new branches worldwide, led to changes in the way it was run. It boosted its profile by taking over the administration of the London Court of Arbitration and through the contribution made by members and staff to the Arbitration Acts of 1979 and 1996. Its rising reputation was recognized by the grant of a Royal Charter in 1979 and the appointment of a succession of distinguished UK judges as Honorary Presidents.

In 1971 David Reid retired after almost a decade's sterling service. He would be the Institute's last part-time Secretary. With more than 2,000 members, of whom nearly half were Fellows, the Council decided a review of the way the Institute was run was long overdue. Following a consultants' report, the Council adopted most of its recommendations. The committee structure was reformed, with the creation of an executive committee, although Council insisted its own powers should remain absolute. Council itself became a more effective body. Although it numbered 28 members, and part of its membership was composed of past presidents and co-opted members, there were places for regional nominated members, and other places were filled through election by postal ballot. The roles of President and Vice-President became honorary, and the post of Chairman of Council was created for the purposes of managing day-to-day business. The Council also agreed to create a small permanent secretariat (at the time the only full-time member of staff was Anne Kenny) under a full-time Secretary to further the Institute's promotion of arbitration in its widest sense worldwide. It was a major step towards creating a more professional organization.

Bertie Vigrass, appointed full-time Secretary of the Institute in 1972.

The soaring popularity of package holidays in the 1970s created a corresponding need for schemes to settle consumer disputes.

The initial appointment of a full-time Secretary proved short-lived but the Council made an inspired choice in then appointing Bertie Vigrass, formerly executive director of the British Institute of Management, to the post from 1 November 1972. It seemed auspicious that almost simultaneously the Institute's first international branch was being formed in Hong Kong. The second key appointment made during the next ten years was that of Kerry Harding as Deputy Secretary in 1981. He would succeed Vigrass in 1986 and together these two men shared much of the responsibility for the development of the Institute between 1972 and 1999.

The expansion of branches in the UK and other countries, accompanied by an expanding membership, covered in the first chapter of this book, was only part of the story of the Institute's development. Although construction disputes still accounted for the majority of arbitrations conducted by members in England and Wales, the Institute took advantage of the consumer age to expand its interest into other areas. The Institute benefited from

the links first made with the Consumer Council in the early 1960s, when it had helped the Motor Agents Association to develop a small claims consumer arbitration scheme. Its success, and the general tendency for consumers to make claims against retailers, led to the creation of a similar scheme on behalf of the travel industry. In 1973 the Office of Fair Trading was established, creating in its Director-General, John Methven, the first consumer watchdog. Methven, a successful lawyer and businessman, realized that these small schemes were the best way of settling many consumer disputes. The package holiday had made foreign travel affordable for many thousands of families and there was a pressing need for a whole of industry scheme for travel operators. When Methven asked the Institute for help, Vigrass and his staff were only too happy to respond. The Institute devised, set up and administered a scheme for the Association of British Travel Agents, the latter covering the costs of arbitrations. Implemented in 1975, this proved so successful that it led to a proliferation of similar schemes under the aegis of the

Presidents' Reception, Middle Temple, London, 1993. Left to right: Lord Bingham, Bruce Harris, John Sims, Francis McWilliams, Lord Donaldson, Ronald Bernstein QC, Geoffrey Beresford Hartwell and Leslie Alexander.

Institute. Eventually totalling almost 60, these schemes not only raised the Institute's profile, and in areas outside construction, but they also provided a welcome revenue stream. They would eventually be eclipsed with the advent of ombudsmen schemes for the resolution of disputes in specific sectors.

The extension of arbitration into consumer fields was symptomatic of its greater use to resolve disputes as commerce grew and contracts became increasingly complex. The situation was summed up by the Institute's President in 1974–5 (the separation of President and Chairman took effect in 1977), Richard Soper:

The issues we cover range from disputes involving sums measured in millions of pounds, whether it be in building or civil engineering disputes or shipping disputes, both in the United Kingdom and abroad, to disputes involving claims for sums measured only in pounds, as in the case of the Institute's Arbitration Scheme for the Travel Industry and the servicing, repair and sales of cars by motor agents, as well as other disputes in the commodity field and in industrial relations.

The success of the Institute's dynamic approach towards arbitration led to its involvement in the revival of another even older English arbitral institution. The London Court of Arbitration (LCA) had been founded in 1892 as the tribunal for the arbitration of domestic and international commercial disputes with their origins in the City. The term

'London Arbitration' had been commonly used for decades in international contracts. But the LCA had declined after 1945, hindered in part by the lack of reform in English arbitration law, and was failing to capitalize on the growth in arbitration as international trade expanded. In 1975 the bodies responsible for administering the LCA, the London Chamber of Commerce and Industry and the City of London Corporation, invited the Institute, which had moved into City offices in Cannon Street, to become part of the joint committee. Vigrass took over the role of Registrar and the Institute merged its existing arbitration activities with the LCA. It was a very successful relationship, thanks in part to the energetic involvement of the Registrar. In 1981, to better reflect the nature of its work, the LCA was renamed as the London Court of International Arbitration (LCIA). With a reformed administration, innovative rules and improvements in English arbitration law, the LCIA prospered once again.

When the LCIA separated from the Institute in 1986, as its workload expanded considerably, Vigrass gave up his post as Secretary and concentrated full-time on his role as LCIA Registrar. The loss of Vigrass was a blow to the Institute, whose profile and membership he had done so much to develop. More particularly, he had always

London's Guildhall, the original home of the LCA.

Coat of Arms

With the Royal Charter, the Institute also obtained a grant of arms. The shield depicted in the arms is divided into eight sections, suggesting the multiplicity of problems facing the arbitrator. The sword and scales represent fair play while the crest of the upper half of a horse bearing a purse and key symbolizes speed, commerce and unlocking solutions. The motto, *Celeriter ac Diligenter*, may be translated as Swiftly and Carefully, encapsulating part of the essence of arbitration. Many of the aspects, including the colours of red and silver, were taken from the arms of the Institute's first Honorary President, Lord Diplock.

been successful in attracting as members UK-based international arbitrators. With the Institute still dominated by construction arbitration in England and Wales, the split made membership less attractive to international arbitrators, many of whom perceived the Institute to be a parochial body. This was a perception the Institute would find difficult to overcome as the domestic construction industry moved from arbitration to statutory adjudication while international commercial arbitration grew rapidly.

A contributory factor to the revival of the LCIA was the reform of English arbitration law. As in the 1930s, the Institute played a central role, and once again one of its members, this time Lord Hacking, helped to steer the legislation through Parliament. There had long been

Honorary Presidents

1977–80: Lord Diplock; 1981–3: Lord Donaldson; 1983–6: Sir Michael Kerr; 1986–91: Lord Goff; 1991–5: Sir Thomas Bingham; 1995–8: Lord Mustill; 1998–2001: Sir Anthony Evans; 2001–5: Lord Fraser of Carmyllie

The post of Honorary President lasted from 1977 until 2005. The Institute was able to persuade some of the finest legal and

Clockwise from top left: Michael Rutherford, Lord Bingham, Lady Bingham and Margaret Rutherford.

arbitral minds among the UK judiciary of the day to take up this office. Lord Diplock, a formidable intellect and outstanding contributor to constitutional and public law, found his name attached to Northern Ireland's Diplock courts, where cases were decided by a judge sitting alone, but he excelled in many different fields of the law, including arbitration. Lord Donaldson was the only president of the UK's ill-fated Industrial Relations Court and presided over the trials of the Guildford Four and the Maguire Seven, notable miscarriages of justice, for which he later incurred criticism. As Master of the Rolls in succession to Lord Denning from 1982, he gained a reputation as a champion of the reform of civil procedure and the extension

of judicial review to hold government to account. Sir Michael Kerr was born in Berlin and came to Britain with his family as a refugee from Nazi Germany. An outstanding barrister, his practice in commercial cases stimulated his interest in commercial arbitration, and he came to believe strongly in the merits of negotiated settlement to solve disputes. He was a popular and successful judge in the Commercial Court before becoming a Lord Justice of Appeal, from which he retired in 1989 to become a full-time international arbitrator. Lord Goff was also a successful barrister, specializing in commercial law, and judge, rising to become the Senior Law Lord in the UK before his retirement in 1998. One of the last cases to come before him was the attempt to extradite General Pinochet. Sir Thomas Bingham, later Lord Bingham, specialized in commercial and public law at the bar, and first sat as a judge in the Commercial Court, before successively becoming Master of the Rolls, Lord Chief Justice and an outstandingly successful Senior Law Lord. He was an enthusiastic advocate of legal reform and sought to make the courtroom much less daunting and more effective. Lord Mustill played a key part in the most recent reform of English arbitration law and sat as chair of the Departmental Committee on the Law of Arbitration. He wrote extensively on commercial arbitration and would also later act as an arbitrator. After serving as a Lord Justice of Appeal, he became a Law Lord in 1992, retiring in 1997. Sir Anthony Evans became a leading international maritime lawyer before becoming a judge, when he sat in the Commercial Court. In 2005 he became the first Chief Justice of the Dubai International Financial Centre Courts. Lord Fraser of Carmyllie combined a successful career as a lawyer with an equally successful political career, serving as Scottish Solicitor General almost continuously between 1982 and 1992. He also became the senior Scottish law officer, Lord Advocate, in 1989, taking over responsibility for the Lockerbie inquiry.

Lord Bingham (second from right) on an Institute panel.

criticism of the way the Special Case procedure was abused, encouraging the intervention of the English judiciary to set aside arbitral awards. This worked to the disadvantage of London as a centre of international arbitration since the possibility of English judges interfering with arbitral awards deterred many overseas businesses. The Arbitration Act, 1979, helped to rectify this situation, and generally overhauled English arbitration law.

This achievement raised the Institute's profile. Combined with continuing growth – in 1979 there were more than 4,000 members across 40 countries – this gave the Institute the confidence to apply once again for the grant of a Royal Charter. John Phillips, a qualified barrister, was instrumental in achieving this long-held objective. As President in 1976–77, he used his presidential address to urge consideration of pursuing a Royal Charter to seal the Institute's reputation as a body with a high public purpose. The Institute petitioned the Queen in December 1977. The process was not unimpeded. Objections from two organizations were overcome thanks largely to Phillips' negotiating skills. The charter was granted on 6 February 1979. It set out clearly the objects of what was now the Chartered Institute of Arbitrators: 'to promote and facilitate the determination of disputes by arbitration; to provide for the appointment of arbitrators for the settlement of disputes; to promote a wider knowledge of the law and practice of arbitration; to consider, originate, support and procure improvements in the law relating to arbitration'. On 6 June 1979 nearly 350 people celebrated the Institute's new status at a reception and supper in Middle Temple.

Phillips was also the driving force, with other senior members such as Clifford Clark, as well as Vigrass, behind the subsequent creation of the Worshipful Company of Arbitrators, which became the 93rd livery company in the City of London on 17 March 1981. Phillips was the first Master, Clark the Senior Warden and Norman Royce, another Past President, the Junior Warden. In 1985

Sir Anthony Evans and Lord Fraser of Carmyllie.

Institute event at Mansion House. Guests include, from the left, Ronald Bernstein QC (3), John Tackaberry QC (4), Lady Goff (5), Lord Goff (7), Maurice Pleasance (9), Margaret Pleasance (10) and Ian Menzies (11).

Phillips also gave the first annual lecture, forming part of the activities of the charity established by the Company for the promotion of education with particular regard to arbitration.

By the time Bertie Vigrass handed over as Secretary to Kerry Harding in 1986, the Institute was a very different organization. It had regained its confidence, raised its profile and trebled its membership. Although it was still an organization dominated by domestic construction arbitration, it was tentatively backing the creation of branches around the world.

There was, however, some concern that in concentrating on creating a more professional body the Institute had lost sight of its primary objective under the Royal Charter. In 1983 Ray Turner, as Chairman, had emphasized that the Institute must constantly be on guard against the erosion of the benefits of arbitration through rising costs and increasing complexity, and remain active in making arbitration more effective and efficient. In 1986 another Chairman, Douglas Stephenson, reported that the Institute was seeking consent to use the term 'Chartered Arbitrator' to signify the status of those serving on the Institute's

arbitration panels. In 1988 the ever cogent Ronald Bernstein pointed out that there were widening opportunities to deploy arbitration in the modern commercial world yet, at the same time, dissatisfaction with arbitration was increasing. The Institute clearly had a job to do.

Yet it was hamstrung by its parlous finances. In 1986, as Harding recalled, money was 'very tight, to put it mildly'. The Institute was living from hand to mouth, relying on an overdraft to cover expenses towards the end of each year before subscriptions were renewed every January. Matters were not helped by the decision in 1990 to take an expensive lease without break clauses on a modern office development (Angel Gate, Islington) remote from the heart of the City. When it had been necessary to vacate the Institute's rather drab offices in Cannon Street, there had been resistance among Council members to acquiring a permanent headquarters, and an opportunity had been missed to take up affordable premises in the Docklands, which was just being developed. It was understandable in the circumstances that a parsimonious attitude was taken towards money, with Harding determined to turn the situation around.

Hence the importance of the Institute's first corporate plan in 1989, critical, felt Kerry Harding, in resetting the Institute's compass. What was needed, according to the plan, was 'a cultural change; a change from an Institute dominated by distinguished individuals pursuing oft-times uncoordinated goals to a properly-staffed and well-managed Institute with members and staff working together harmoniously'.

For the Institute to carry out its objectives, its finances had to be put in order. How to achieve this was a central part of the plan. More subscription revenue was essential. The expansion of international commercial arbitration went hand in hand with greater global commerce, bringing more members every year to an Institute recognized as the only arbitral body offering qualifications valid worldwide.

This helped the number of members to increase from just over 6,000 in the early 1980s to some 9,000 in the late 1990s. On the one hand, this eased financial pressures, but on the other, activities and staff were expanding to meet the needs of more members scattered across the world. Through careful financial management, sound tax planning and additional income from increased commercial activities, coupled with more and more members, matters steadily improved. When Harding first joined the Institute in 1981, there had been £16,000 in the bank; when he retired in 1999, total funds stood at £2.5m. This would help his successor to move the Institute into its first permanent home.

The senior member with the task of overseeing the implementation of the corporate plan was Geoffrey King, as Chairman of Council responsible for the day-to-day business of the Institute in association with the Secretary General and his team. King also kept a close eye on the Institute's finances. The post was occupied by a succession of leading arbitrators during the 1990s. It was a time of some tension, Harding recollected, between the more cautious older generation and a younger generation impatient for change. Of the latter, John Tackaberry was among the vanguard. He was eager to alter the complexion of the Institute's members and made a plea for the

Margaret Rutherford with Lord Denning, 1982.

recruitment of additional younger members and more women, where the Institute had always been weak. Two years later the first woman was elected to chair the Council. Margaret Rutherford, a leading barrister, was one of only three women on the Council, one of whom, Karen Gough, would become President in 2001, the second youngest holder of the office. (Teresa Cheng would also take up the position in 2008–9.) Rutherford worked hard to bring in more female members, arranging a variety of events to encourage their participation, with some success, although the number of female members has remained small.

Throughout this period the Institute and its members were once again engaged in improving English arbitration law. In 1976 the United Nations Commission on International Trade Law (UNCITRAL) agreed Model Rules for Arbitration, which in turn led to the adoption of a Model Law in 1985. The Institute advised the British government on the negotiations that led to the Model Law, which, although it was not adopted by Britain, influenced the Arbitration Act of 1996. Senior members of the Institute contributed much to legislation that helped to move English arbitration closer to international practice.

Margaret Rutherford, the first woman elected to chair the Council.

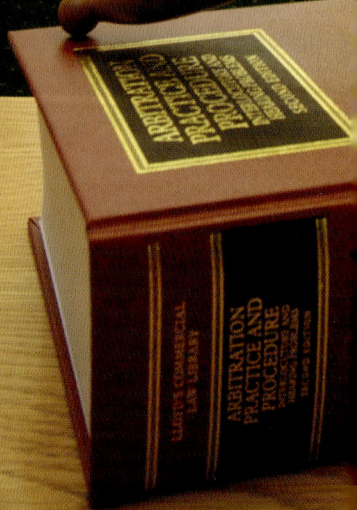

Part 3

ARBITRATION, ADR AND EDUCATION

8

ARBITRATION AND THE ARBITRATORS

The expansion of trade has driven the growing use of arbitration since the early 1900s and particularly since 1945. Interest in developing an international framework for arbitration first began in the 1920s and is still underway today. The general acceptance of arbitration in international commerce has also brought challenges to ensure that the way arbitration is practised remains relevant and helpful for the users. In turn this places a premium on the role of the Institute in continuing to develop a pool of qualified, skilled, experienced and knowledgeable arbitrators worldwide.

As a result of the unrivalled reach of British imperial trade, the English system of arbitration came to dominate the commercial world by the late nineteenth century. Moreover, arbitration as practised in other parts of the world, such as France and the United States, suffered even greater judicial hostility than in Britain. Then, as now, arbitration in the English-speaking world concentrated on disputes relating mainly to construction, shipping and commodities.

Ian Hunter QC, Michael Black QC and John Hinchey at an India branch event in Delhi, 2010.

The growing use of commercial arbitration made clarifying and consolidating the law ever more urgent. Partly through the efforts of the Corporation of the City of London and the London Chamber of Commerce, who saw such legislation as a way of fostering trade, the Arbitration Act, 1889, effectively divided arbitration between that ordered by the courts and that voluntarily entered into by the parties in dispute. More and more commercial contracts began to include arbitration clauses. The Chamber of Shipping first issued standard contracts with arbitration clauses around 1890, with other bodies, such as the London Corn Trade Association and the Oil Seed Association, soon following suit. Arbitration was also extended to disputes involving insurance companies and friendly societies. London became popular for commercial arbitration and the Commercial Court was created in 1895. By the early 1920s Chaplin Baldwin could write in the Institute's journal that 'Arbitration is more definitely established in Great Britain than it is in any other country in the world, and although the actual practice is confined in the main to certain trades, the machinery is complete and has been fully tested and is ready, whether industrially or professionally.'

The British Empire in 1886. The unrivalled reach of imperial trade resulted in the domination of the English system of arbitration.

Even so, for many years the English legal profession was openly hostile to arbitration. A typical attack was apparently penned by a judge in an anonymous article in *The Times* in August 1892. The author referred to

the hazardous and mysterious chances of arbitration, in which some arbitrator, who knows as much about the law as he does about theology, by the application of a rough and ready moral consciousness, or upon the affable principle of dividing the victory equally between both sides, decides intricate questions of law and fact with equal ease. The one supreme attraction which draws merchants and traders into the circle of such grotesque justice is that it is prompt, that it is cheap, that there are ... 'no fresh fields and pastures new' of litigation, stretching in interminable prospect.

Similar attacks were being made 30 years later, this time more openly. In 1921, for instance, an English county court judge criticized what he called 'home-made tribunals' and asserted that the courts were quicker, cheaper and more effective. This was a claim robustly disputed by the Institute's journal, which pointed to the many merchants and traders who would never dare enter a courtroom on even the smallest commercial matter without taking extensive and expensive legal advice. The pages of the Institute's journal were filled with horror stories about the cost of taking disputes to court.

One of the reasons judges and lawyers poured scorn on arbitration in the early life of the Institute was the inadequacy of too many arbitrators. The professional arbitrator had begun to emerge at the end of the nineteenth century out of the tribunal system operated in the City of London. But too many cases attracted bad publicity because

59

Developing highly skilled arbitrators worldwide: members' meeting in Singapore.

of the poor performance of the arbitrators. They were accused of charging excessive fees, of disregard for natural justice, and for running hearings entirely to suit their own convenience. Where arbitration proved ineffective, a 1922 journal editorial concluded, it had generally been through the appointment of 'a person who may be educated and may occupy socially or commercially a suitable status, but who has had absolutely no training or experience in the often very complicated duties and functions of an arbitrator'. As a consequence, while arbitration had been intended to be a more flexible way of resolving disputes

than resorting to the courts, any advantages it might have had were often negated by the inadequate training and knowledge of many arbitrators. It also frequently left final awards surrounded by uncertainty because of doubts about the arbitrator's legal knowledge.

Then there were cases where arbitrators were too weak to impose any discipline on proceedings, allowing them to be dominated by the counsel representing the parties and resulting in unnecessary expense and delay. One Institute member highlighted in the journal in 1924 a case where a solicitor and barrister were both in attendance, observing that 'the Arbitrator seemed to be in holy terror of the latter, hardly opening his lips throughout the whole of the proceedings'. The writer continued: 'Like most things, arbitration is essentially a simple thing in itself, but the more experience one obtains in such cases the more one realizes that simplicity of the proceedings is the offspring of knowledge and aptitude on the part of the Arbitrator'.

Sometimes delays were caused by arbitrators whose other commitments prevented a speedy resolution of the case in hand. Sir Illtyd Thomas, a distinguished surveyor, recounted in the journal in 1931 a notorious mining arbitration that illustrated just this point, as well as the consequences of appointing an arbitrator in haste without considering whether he was right for the job. An arbitrator had been chosen for the case but died within ten days. 'Another barrister of great repute … was then agreed upon, and the proceedings recommenced upon a journey so long, that people often wondered if death would again intervene'. The arbitrator sat for short periods, usually after the courts had risen in London, over the course of 200 days, partly because the claimant was litigious and called an inordinate number of witnesses. More than 80 years later, similar criticisms are still being made, with one arbitrator citing a case where the parties were happy to appoint as arbitrator a lawyer who had told them that he would not have the time even for a telephone conversation for two and a half years.

The Institute was founded to tackle problems such as these and in so doing to elevate the status and reputation of the arbitrator. The Institute repeatedly stressed the characteristics required by any reputable arbitrator. The very first edition of the journal emphasized that 'a business experience, unassailable integrity, entire freedom from bias or partiality, and a desire to do justice to both parties constituted a complete qualification for the position of an arbitrator'. An article in 1923 listed not only the knowledge the best arbitrators should possess but also the duties they needed to observe. Essential knowledge included an experience and understanding of the profession or trade involved, as well as knowledge of the relevant law, including

the law governing arbitration. Duties included even-handed treatment of the parties and their evidence, confining any judgement to the evidence they gave and the documents they presented, and making careful and clear awards to avoid any misunderstanding. In addition, an arbitrator should also possess an understanding of human nature, self-confidence, integrity, tact, patience and a sense of humour. It was a demanding specification. And time after time members robustly defended the advantages of arbitration; as one member insisted in 1938, 'We believe that arbitration is an expeditious, economical and efficient method of settling disputes … The essence of arbitration, international or individual, is that the parties should be brought together at the earliest opportunity, in a congenial atmosphere, and a fair settlement expeditiously sought'.

The shortcomings of the Arbitration Act, 1889, exacerbated the failings of some arbitrators. For example,

Sir Illtyd Thomas, 1930.

it was evident that the 'Special Case' enshrined in the Act had significant disadvantages. Certainly the submission of 'Special Cases' before the courts helped to stimulate the development of commercial law. They also clarified the law for the arbitrator and for the parties, assisted judges to ensure the uniform application of the law and, because such judgements became public, unlike arbitration awards, which were confidential, set precedents for future arbitrations. But the downside was the time and money involved, which often led to considerable delays in making an award. Arbitrators with incomplete legal knowledge, recorded an early version of the journal, faced with difficulties resulting from their ignorance of the law, leaned too often on the 'Special Case', which became the rule

The House of Lords, photgraphed in 1993 – the following year it was to be the scene of Askwith's triumph with the amended Arbitration Act.

rather than the exception, leading to an excessive reliance upon the principle of legality rather than equity. The article emphasized that 'special knowledge, training and experience, together with an acquaintance with the laws of evidence, the rules for construction of written documents, the principles of law and equity, and some degree of judicial capacity, are equally important'. As commercial matters became increasingly complex, it was contended, membership of the Institute should become a guarantee of integrity, independence, objectivity and professionalism.

There were other weaknesses in the English system. Some contracts made it impossible for the injured party to take legal action unless an arbitration award had first been made, which put some cases outside the statute of limitations. There were clauses that no claim was valid unless arbitration had been commenced within an absurdly short period, leaving many overseas parties complaining that this left them too little time to bring their disputes. Too often arbitrators found themselves unpaid by a failure to stipulate payment from the parties at the outset.

As trade expanded once more after the end of the First World War, there was also a renewed need to consolidate the law. As early as 1922 the Institute was pressing for the ever-expanding web of legislation covering English arbitration to be brought together in one act. The reference in many invitations to arbitrate often failed to make clear under which provision the arbitration should be decided, with the result that, as *The Arbitrator* observed in July 1922, 'all this mass of varying provisions is embarrassing to any arbitrator called upon professionally to deal with widely different sources of dispute'.

The Institute's interest in reform persisted throughout the 1920s and in the early 1930s resulted in legislation. Under the influence of the President, Lord Askwith, the Institute formed a special committee that made innumerable recommendations to the government for amending the 1889 Act. When the government pleaded lack of time to draft a bill, the Institute took up the challenge instead. A group of senior members, including

Dispute Appointment Service convention, 2013.

Askwith, Colonel F. N. Falkner, J. R. W. Alexander, V. Aronson and R. S. Fraser, together with the Institute's part-time Secretary and his part-time staff, was almost entirely responsible for drafting what became the Arbitration Act, 1934, piloted by Askwith through the House of Lords. In addition to consolidating existing law, it also gave arbitrators the power to order the specific performance of contracts and make interim awards.

As well as domestic arbitration, international arbitration expanded enormously during the interwar years.

By 1928, as one newspaper was reported as saying in *The Arbitrator*, 'The great value of international arbitration in foreign trade has been increasingly appreciated since the war'. These views were echoed by the Institute's President, H. B. Chaplin Baldwin, at the Institute's first annual dinner in the same year:

> Thanks to the marvels of telephony and wireless, all foreign countries, even foreign continents, are brought to our doorsteps, and in consequence the trade in which we are now engaged was infinitely more world-wide than ever it has been in its history. Was it not inevitable that in the carrying out of such an immense volume of trade there must arise perfectly natural misunderstanding, disputes which in themselves had no legal significance whatever, matters purely of fact, possibly merely of interpretation, often of opinion, but vitally affecting the business in question? All these matters, in their opinion, were essentially ones which should be dealt with by means of arbitration.

During the 1920s the first steps were taken towards universal rules for international arbitration, although this journey would only be completed with the New York Convention of 1958. When the International Chamber of Commerce (ICC) met in Rome in 1923, delegates stressed the need for international arbitration clauses to be respected, for international uniformity in the practice of arbitration, and for the universal enforcement of international arbitration awards. The result was the formation of the ICC Court of Arbitration in the same year. Also in 1923 the League of Nations issued a protocol on arbitration, which bound signatories to enforce arbitration awards in their own jurisdictions in accordance with their own laws. Representatives of international trades negotiated their own arbitration agreements, such as the one agreed in 1926 by the representatives of the English, French, Belgian, German and Italian wool textile industries. In the following year, the Geneva Convention was agreed, enabling awards made under the original protocol to be enforced in a ratifying state under certain conditions. By 1939 more than 50 states had signed the convention. The Institute journal described the protocol as 'a friendly gesture to overcome a possible conflict of laws in different subscribing states' and a method of allowing merchants to trade internationally with confidence. The weakness of the system was that it failed as a matter of course to cover the enforcement in one country of an award made in another and left undisturbed the precedence of each state's own arbitration laws and procedures.

The cooperation between countries outside the British sphere of influence inevitably led to a movement

The opening session of the League of Nations, Geneva, 1922.

for the adoption of civil law as the basis for a standard international commercial arbitration agreement. The British only slowly woke up to this development but the eventual realization galvanized the Institute into working for the wider recognition of common law in international arbitration. The British antipathy towards civil law was set out by Sir Lynden Macassey in 1945, when he pointed out that the practice in many civil law countries, where the arbitrator might act as a conciliator, deciding whatever they considered to be fair, flew in the face of the sanctity of the contract for British businessmen. This had led many British trade associations, such as the London Corn Trade Association, the Incorporated Oil Seed Association and the London Jute Association, to draw up and administer their own arbitration procedures enshrined in standard forms of contract. Tens of thousands of cases were handled by these associations even though they remained unenforceable overseas. The argument would rumble on until the end of the century.

The state of international commercial arbitration on the verge of the Second World War was summed up many years later by Lord Wilberforce:

Lord Wilberforce, 1969.

> It was a simpler world that existed before 1939, when the early editions of *Russell on Arbitration* were being written, when the simple laws on arbitration were being drafted, a world in which trade was freely taking place between a limited number of reasonably solvent western nations; when charter parties, commodity contracts and rules as to carriage by sea or by land were generally understood and generally applied, when borrowing contracts, even those resulting from World War I, were drawn up in a legal form with provision which were expected to be carried out, with default provision which were enforced if they were not. International arbitration of course existed: it had its institutional background: the London Court of Arbitration, the American Association, the ICC, were all there and being used, but quite a slim volume could have encompassed all the law.

All this, as Wilberforce went on to point out, changed enormously with the explosion in international trade after 1945. With more trading nations, more states directly involved in overseas trade, the application of a wider array of diverse national legal systems and a more complicated financial environment, arbitration became increasingly preferred to litigation, especially when taking action in the wrong jurisdiction could be commercially disastrous. The hegemony of the London trade associations and their standard contracts was swept away by the vast increase in complex one-off contracts.

In 1945 the main challenge for international arbitration was that awards were still unenforceable in many countries. The Institute's President, Sir Lynden Macassey, was passionate on the subject. Speaking in 1945, he told members that a general system of international arbitration was essential, incorporating common arbitration rules, a standard arbitration clause, universally enforced awards, national panels of suitably qualified arbitrators and international supervision.

Macassey was critical of the backwardness of English arbitration law, which by the late 1940s was seen as a major hindrance to English exporters. He highlighted the law's principal weakness, which was that any award always remained subject to judicial intervention regardless of whether the parties had agreed it should be final, binding and not subject to legal review. English law was out of step with the law not only in the US but in many other countries. It deterred parties from coming to London to settle their disputes.

In 1946 Macassey highlighted the example set by the American Arbitration Association (AAA), whose influence had brought about a common system of commercial arbitration throughout North America and Latin America. Macassey suggested that as an initial step on the road to a standard international system there should be a reciprocal agreement between the Institute and the AAA to enable any dispute arising in the US, Canada or Latin America to be arbitrated according to AAA rules and in England under Institute rules. The AAA went further and in 1947 reached a reciprocal agreement with the ICC. In England, however, the Institute missed its opportunity. It was the LCA, the sole UK participant in the ICC's International Commercial Arbitration Committee set up in 1946, with which the AAA reached a limited mutual arbitration agreement in 1947.

Macassey cannot have made himself overly popular with the Institute's members by his constant reference to the AAA's influence and the more central role that arbitration played in the US, where, he said, it was seen as 'a public matter, a way of life, a habit of thought, a part of the essential machinery of characteristic American business, a vital element in the democratic way of doing things'. He also contrasted the support given to arbitration by the US legal profession with the disdain in which it was held by many English lawyers, who rather saw it as an intrusion into the law.

By 1950 the United Nations had established an international law commission, tasked among other things

Edmund F. Becker, Jr, of the United States and N. G. C. Pearson of the United Kingdom at the UN Conference on International Commercial Arbitration, New York, 1958.

Clifford Clark, a maritime arbitrator and a driving force behind the Worshipful Company of Arbitrators.

with devising an international arbitration system. Eventually this initiative led to the UN Conference on International Commercial Arbitration held in New York in June 1958, which resulted in the Convention on the Recognition and Enforcement of Foreign Arbitral Awards. As the name suggests, it provided for the enforcement of an award in a country other than that where the award was made. The Convention was ratified by a growing number of states (53 by 1979, 148 by 2012), including all the major trading nations, although it was not until 1975 that it was ratified by the UK. This was surprising for the Convention made London-based international arbitration even less attractive, as an award based on a 'Special Case' decided by the court could be held to have arisen through judicial interference and ran the risk of being refused recognition in another country where assets were held by the losing party.

The damage this caused English arbitration was exemplified by the remarks made in the late 1970s to Lord Hacking by the general counsel for a major US company, who said that he had instructed his team never again to agree to the UK as a venue for arbitration. This stimulated Hacking, a qualified barrister and experienced international arbitrator, to take up the cause of reform. He found other members, such as Clifford Clark, a leading maritime arbitrator, were also eager for change and only too willing

to help. In 1977 a joint committee was formed, comprising representatives of the Institute, the London Maritime Arbitrators Association and the LCA.

The need for reform became more urgent with the adoption of the UNCITRAL Model Rules in 1976, drafted

The Arbitrator's Style

John Cane, *Arbitration*, February 1986

Arbitration could often be less than glamorous. Cane recounted one case held in the middle of a blizzard in an unheated village cricket pavilion, with everyone in wellington boots, overcoats and scarves; while another was held in an old, small town hall lacking ancillary rooms, 'so that Counsel had to settle the matter in the gents' toilet, whilst the arbitrator sat on the stairs outside, wondering whether it would ever end'. Sometimes arbitrators had to resort to extreme action. 'Very occasionally the arbitrator may be obliged to quell violence which breaks out, and very enjoyable that is when it occurs. Long dormant skills, learned in old unhappy far-off days and battles long ago, will be called into play. I once helped an arbitrator as he stood in his wrecked office. He seemed twenty years younger. They submitted to him humbly in the future and the cost of breakages went on the bill.'

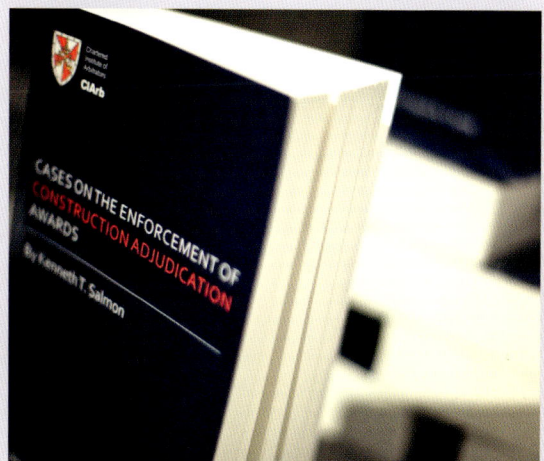

at the request of developing countries to rebalance an international arbitration system dominated by rules devised by developed nations for arbitrations largely taking place in, and under the administration of, arbitrators from developed nations. The Rules had been widely accepted by many countries in the developed and developing world and had been taken into account by the LCA in revising its own rules in 1978. At the same time many other countries were already reforming their own arbitration law as they competed to attract the business arising from international arbitration, with regional arbitration centres springing up all over the globe. The LCA, or LCIA as it became, the ICC and the AAA all flourished, and the International Federation of Commercial Arbitration Institutions was formed.

Bertie Vigrass worked assiduously with others for the reform of English law. They persuaded an array of influential

Arbitration in the US

The New York Chamber of Commerce formed an arbitration committee in 1768, but despite several attempts to enshrine arbitration in law during the nineteenth century this was achieved only in 1920. In fact, arbitration was regarded with suspicion and hostility by the legal profession in most US states until that time. In 1925 federal arbitration legislation was passed, yet even in 1931 arbitration clauses in contracts were irrevocable and enforceable in only ten US states. The American Arbitration Association (AAA) was formed from three separate organizations in 1926. Within a year the AAA had nearly 1,000 members and by 1941 it had 7,000 members spread across 1,600 towns and cities. The AAA had an international vision, and foresaw the harmonization of international rules governing arbitration, but within the US there was limited growth in commercial arbitration, which was still not widely recognized by the early 1960s. This began to change. In 1970 the New York Convention became part of US law and in 1984 the Supreme Court upheld the supremacy of the Federal Arbitration Act over any state statutes denying enforcement of an arbitration clause in interstate contracts.

The US Supreme Court.

peers with distinguished judicial experience, including Lord Denning, Lord Hailsham and Lord Rawlinson, to back the motion for reform Hacking was submitting for debate in the House of Lords in May 1978. The lingering doubts harboured about the proposal by another distinguished law lord, Lord Diplock, could have posed a problem, but several people began a campaign to persuade him to change his mind, including Vigrass, who, wrote Hacking many years later in the Institute's journal, 'had Lord Diplock made the President of the Institute, and by this means, got into an inner track to him. It worked!' The support of these judicial heavyweights helped to convince the government of the day of the merits of the case as the proposals made their way through Parliament during 1978–9. Denning and Hailsham would become honorary members of the Institute. The legislation was almost lost when the government succumbed to a vote of confidence in April 1979. It was only saved through its inclusion in an agreement to pass non-contentious legislation on the nod just hours before the government resigned.

Hacking contended that the Arbitration Act 1979 had a bigger impact than its limited provisions, which moved the emphasis firmly but not entirely away from judicial intervention. The English judiciary, however, interpreted the passage of the Act, Hacking wrote in 1986, 'as representing a shift in public policy relating to arbitrations from an insistence on strict legality to the recognition of the need of commercial efficacy, speed and finality'. In effect, it represented the final acceptance by English lawyers of the place of arbitration within the legal system. Two important legal decisions soon after the passage of the Act confirmed this interpretation: in the Bremer Vulcan case (1981) the courts decided that they had no power to intervene when the arbitrator or the parties had the necessary powers for the proper conduct of proceedings; in the case of the Nema (1981), the judges severely limited the grounds of appeal to the courts. This certainty helped to rebuild confidence in English arbitration law and contributed significantly to the LCIA's revival.

The Act was held up by one of the world's leading experts on arbitration, Professor Pieter Sanders, as a good example of how governments could begin to harmonize arbitration law. Speaking at an international conference jointly organized by the Institute, the AAA and Arbitrators' Institute of Canada in Bermuda in 1980, Sanders also pointed to the continuing problem in finding well-trained, experienced and reputable arbitrators to administer the new system. The Institute's own role in meeting this need, he said, was 'exemplary'.

Following the adoption of the Model Rules, negotiations began on drawing up a Model Law. Opinion within the Institute – and the world of English arbitration – was divided over the merits of the proposed Law. At a symposium organized by the Institute in 1983, Mr Justice Mustill (later Lord Justice Mustill) argued that the principal advantage of a Model Law lay in its potential universality, making it easier to deal with transnational disputes, when international trade had been isolated from any particular system of law. He also put his finger on the reason for English scepticism towards the Model Law: it was based not on common law but on civil law. The UK, he said, had only itself to blame for its failure to properly engage with

Lord Mustill, 1998.

the process of international arbitration regulation until it was too late.

An editorial in the Institute journal in August 1983, however, had pointed out that many members were themselves questioning the place of adversarial systems, epitomized by common law, in commercial arbitration. In a consumer age, it was all about keeping customers happy, the editorial continued. 'We must never fail to keep uppermost in mind how essential it is, in the private arbitration service, to maintain a keen eye on the need to achieve consumer satisfaction.' The article was confident that 'the remould of English arbitral procedures brought about by pressures from without inexorably will be an improvement on present practices'.

In his address to the Institute's conference in Guernsey in 1984, Lord Wilberforce, another distinguished British judge, noted the hostility of the UK authorities to the constraints the Model Law imposed on judicial intervention. Drawing on the New York Convention, the Law prohibited intervention during arbitration, curtailed powers to set aside awards for misconduct, and prevented any review on issues of law. Wilberforce noted that the Model Law was bound to be widely adopted and hoped that a compromise acceptable to the UK might be reached.

His words fell on fertile ground. Over the next couple of years members of the Institute organized workshops and

Arbitration in Africa

The UNCITRAL Model Law was widely embraced in many parts of Africa. Zimbabwe, for example, adopted the Model Law as its own arbitration law in 1996, whereas South Africa adopted the Model Law for international commercial arbitration while reforming its own earlier legislation for domestic arbitration. In countries like Swaziland, the pressure for change came from the recognition that existing legislation was inadequate to deal with the rising number of major engineering and construction projects taking place. This was also the pattern in countries like Nigeria and Ghana, where changes to state dispute resolution arrangements came in response to massive inward investment. Several international arbitration centres also opened in places such as Kigali, Lagos, Mauritius and Nairobi.

held seminars on the Model Law and sent representatives to meetings of UNCITRAL in Vienna. In fact, the Institute was the only non-governmental organization to be granted observer status during deliberations on the Model Law. It was thanks principally to the Institute that the version of the Model Law adopted on 21 June 1985 proved more acceptable to the UK government. The Secretary of State for Trade and Industry, Norman Tebbit, wrote to thank the Institute: 'The Institute's work has been a model of how a representative body can help the Government bring international work to the notice of the public and enable us to formulate our policy.'

The next decision for the UK was whether or not to adopt the Model Law. This led to Mr Justice Mustill's 1989 report. While recommending that the UK should give due weight to the Model Law, rather than attempt to integrate it into existing English arbitration law, the report also concluded that the latter had become so uncertain and unclear that further reform was needed. Senior members of the Institute, such as Arthur Marriott, were once again involved in the process. The Arbitration Act, 1996, sought

Arbitration in Africa: the Lagos Court of Arbitration.

to restate the law of arbitration with clarity, increase the powers of the arbitrator and reduce unnecessary delays or expense in resolving pursuits fairly and impartially.

The Act reflected the trend towards the convergence of common law with civil law in international arbitration. The unflinching belief in the superiority of common law that had characterized the English approach to arbitration disappeared. There was a consensus that arbitrators could learn from best practice from both systems. The globalization of trade brought a recognition that there was also much to learn from the practices pursued in different cultures. Lord Hacking succinctly summed up the character of modern international arbitration in 2003:

> Parties from different jurisdictions with different laws from different cultures using different

Arbitration in the Asia-Pacific

The development of the Asia-Pacific as a centre of international arbitration, based on the huge growth in trade, was focused on Hong Kong and Singapore. International arbitration centres were opened in Hong Kong in 1985 and Singapore in 1991. In 2010 Hong Kong incorporated the Model Law to create a unitary scheme covering both domestic and international arbitration. The position of both centres was boosted by many cases involving Chinese companies since arbitration in China was hindered by restrictions on the ability of external arbitral bodies to administer cases. In Malaysia an international arbitration centre was opened in Kuala Lumpur in 1978 and the country had adopted the Model Law in 2006, encouraging a sea change in the attitude of the judiciary towards the enforcement of awards. Australia was also becoming a viable alternative to other established centres.

The Singapore International Arbitration Centre.

Melbourne, home of Australia's first international centre for commercial arbitration.

Arbitration in Australia had fallen into disrepute by the early 1970s through the lack of experienced and knowledgeable arbitrators. Its revival came through its widespread adoption by the Australian construction industry, and the creation of a pool of reputable arbitrators drawn from members of the Institute. This led to the formation of the Institute of Arbitrators Australia in 1975 and the creation of Australia's first international centre for commercial arbitration in Melbourne. A uniform arbitration act was adopted in each Australian state and also permitted arbitrators to resolve disputes by methods other than arbitration, notably conciliation, widely practised in neighbouring trading nations. In 2010 an international disputes centre was opened in Sydney under Doug Jones as President. India too had adopted the Model Law and reforms were being proposed to restrict the ability of the courts to interfere in cases.

Asia-Pacific event.

languages and different dispute resolution practices, all come together with the commitment to resolve disputes. The good practice of arbitration produces a blending of laws and procedures best suited to resolve the dispute in question. The English Common Law is blended with the Continental Civil Law. Western cultures are blended with eastern cultures. Arbitration, too, when well conducted, is informal and civilized.

Although the 1996 Act was regarded by some as an essentially conservative piece of legislation, its flexible interpretation by the English judiciary (as had happened with the previous 1979 Act) nevertheless resulted in the modernization of English arbitration law as well as its progressive harmonization with international practice. In 1998 Sir Michael Kerr reflected in the journal how the Act 'preaches total flexibility and relative informality'. But, he continued, effective arbitration also required the appointment of high calibre arbitrators, and enlightened lawyers representing the parties. Arbitrators, he said, 'must be cosmopolitan and international in their outlook, not adversarial, and never advocates. They should represent the embodiment of personalized justice'.

The Act certainly encouraged arbitrators to become more flexible, to take greater control of proceedings and to ensure matters were handled expeditiously. The Institute had already been encouraging such an approach. In a lecture in 1995, Ronald Bernstein had recommended better training to enable arbitrators to manage cases more effectively. In the same year, delivering the Bill Tompkins Memorial Lecture, Professor John Uff, a Fellow of the Institute, pointed out that while procedure was at the heart of arbitration, English procedure was not widely admired, making it imperative to persist with the search for alternatives which help to speed up arbitration and make it more efficient, factors entirely within the orbit of the arbitrator.

The art of case management was becoming an essential tool of the arbitrator in the modern era. There were many reasons for this. In some ways arbitration had become a victim of its own success in the post-war world. It became the vehicle of choice for the resolution of commercial disputes in international trade. As the latter expanded, cases almost inevitably became more complex and certainly much more valuable. In many instances the parties involved had much to lose. Lord Mustill, writing in 1989, believed this had changed the nature of arbitration. In previous times, he wrote, 'the participants in a trade dispute would submit it in a good spirit to arbitration, looking for a resolution which would be quick, cheap and informal, and for a decision which would be inspired by practical common sense and a personal knowledge of the trade, and which the loser would accept whether he agreed with it or not'. He doubted whether this spirit was evident any more in many cases. 'Depressing as the task may be, perhaps we should face up to the new set of problems posed by an aggressively confrontational spirit in contemporary arbitration.'

Fellow of the Institute Professor John Uff, with Trinidad and Tobago President George Maxwell Richards, 2010.

Among the problems mentioned by Lord Mustill, one that concerned many arbitrators was the growing tendency to import the procedures and processes of the courtroom. Lord Donaldson, a previous Honorary President of the Institute, had suggested in 1984 that 'Arbitration is usually no more and no less than litigation in the private sector'. Writing in the journal in August 1985, the legal correspondent of the *Financial Times*, A. H. Hermann, described how the involvement of lawyers, brought in whenever interpretation of a contract became an issue, made arbitration little different from litigation. As cases became costlier and more time-consuming, confidentiality was the only remaining advantage. The answer, he believed, lay partly in the hands of the arbitrator. They needed to relinquish the usually passive role they adopted in adversarial proceedings and adopt a more positive approach to managing cases. This opinion had already been voiced by the Chairman of the Institute's Council, Frank Rehder, in May 1985, when he said that 'It is for arbitrators to take hold of their cases, and for solicitors and counsel to co-operate, and to accept that there will be change'.

These were not new arguments. In 1934 the Institute journal had blamed rising delays and costs on the tendency for some parties to fight every small point. In the early 1960s Leslie Alexander, a renowned and experienced arbitrator and past President of the Institute, criticized the baleful influence of the legal profession. Since the parties themselves were responsible for determining the course of proceedings, the arbitrator, he believed, should try to educate them, and their lawyers, about arbitration's innate flexibility. Yet too often he found lawyers resistant to moving away from the quasi-legal procedures that were often the cause of delays, such as their predilection for deluging cases with unnecessary documentation. In fact, lawyers, he found, were only too ready to challenge the arbitrator. He cited one case where counsel had threatened to report him for misconduct after Alexander had insisted that the seating plan was a matter for him and not counsel to decide.

Arbitrator's Casebook

John Campbell QC

John Campbell witnessed his first arbitration take place between his Scottish sheep-farmer father and the buyer of some of his sheep. 'The buyer and my father had not been able to agree on a price, but they knew they wanted to sell and to buy, and had at least agreed that much. Whether that was really a contract, or just an "agreement to agree", was a moot point, but they were going to trade ... The Agreement to Arbitrate was a handwritten letter signed by them both and sent to the local auctioneer. He was to fix the price. Both men knew and trusted him; his experience, his knowledge of the breed, and above all his independence. There would have been no other way to resolve the disagreement. And in due course he came to the farm, walked over the sheep, poking here with his stick and touching and testing there with his hand. After a bit he was taken inside, and put in the dining room with a bottle of Morangie (or perhaps a cup of tea but that seems less likely!) and he wrote his Award, fixing the price of the sheep. I was sent for a twopenny stamp, and watched as with great solemnity he signed his signature over the stamp (that being a requirement of the Stamp Duty laws of those times). Both farmers were happy and the "Great Man" went on his way. His fee was thirty shillings and the case took three or four hours (allowing time for the craic as well!).'

The same arguments persist today. Many arbitral institutions, including the LCIA and the ICC, have revised their rules to encourage greater flexibility, minimize delay and obviate the risks involved in what has been described as 'litigation as total warfare'. Yet many arbitrators find that the parties, despite exercising complete control over the form of proceedings, often insist on taking the longest, most complex and costly route despite contrary advice from the arbitrator they themselves have appointed. The parties, particularly the respondent parties, and their legal counsel, will often attempt to delay or disrupt proceedings or even remove the arbitrator, the result being soaring costs and extended hearings. As John Wilding wrote in the Institute's journal in 2008, 'Dispute resolution is often used more as a weapon than a means of overcoming disagreement'. Even when arbitrators do attempt to expedite proceedings, they are often challenged by the parties. In the words of Nael Bunni, a distinguished international arbitrator with considerable experience, 'You are walking on a tightrope; if you slip one way, you could end up with the whole arbitration being denied'. Today arbitrators in many countries, notably in Europe, have adopted a broader and more positive approach to case management, sometimes pursuing mediation hand in hand with arbitration, or assisting the parties to reach a negotiated settlement without acting as formal mediators.

Cases can still be time-consuming – one arbitrator interviewed for this book was involved in an arbitration just reaching its third anniversary – and the role of the arbitrator as a case manager has been enshrined in the ICC's latest rules. Case management is seen as critical for the effective, timely and inexpensive resolution of disputes, and thus critical for the future of arbitration. But, as Doug Jones pointed out, the tension between a forensic examination of the evidence by the parties and the desire to achieve a speedy and economical solution seems incapable of ever being resolved. Ultimately arbitration delivers a final and binding decision and the main priority must always be on getting this right.

Essentially this translated into a concern, always upheld within the Institute, to ensure that the interests of the parties were paramount. As complex arbitration cases consumed more time and money, there was a growing chorus within the profession to remember that arbitration existed to meet the needs of the parties. In 1983, for instance, Ray

Turner had reminded members that 'arbitration exists to provide a service, not primarily to provide an income for arbitrators, lawyers and experts'. In 1986 an editorial in the journal argued that the profession should always have at the forefront of its mind 'the overriding commitment to service the needs of the consumer engaged both in national and international business activity'. Arbitration, concluded the journal, must offer the consumer 'a truly multi-disciplinary approach to problem-solving coupled with a transnational outlook which can accommodate the wide range of needs of the international business community'.

As increasingly complex cases became more legalistic, costly and time-consuming, this plea was heard from consumers themselves. In 2008, for instance, Michael McIlwrath and Roland Schroeder, senior counsel for General Electric, wrote in the journal that 'international arbitration institutions and professionals should be more mindful of the goals and objectives of businesses that are customers of dispute resolution services'. Asserting that their views were widely shared in business, they complained about the length of time taken to reach an award, when

Jeffrey Elkinson.

Arbitrator's Casebook

Jeffrey Elkinson

The case began in the British Virgin Islands in 2003. It related to a share purchase option in MegaFon, a major Russian telecoms operator, bought for Elkinson's client for $300m. The purchase was challenged by IPOC, a Bermudan mutual fund owned by the Russian minister of telecommunications, which insisted it was entitled to buy the option for $20m. The contract provided for arbitration under ICC Rules in Geneva, Zurich and Stockholm. The case only concluded in Bermuda in 2007, by which time there had been many hearings in many jurisdictions, allegations of perjury and corruption and the disappearance of the individual who had sold the option (he was never found). The value of the shares had also risen to £3.5bn.

an earlier decision on a critical issue could have made a fundamental difference to the direction of the particular company. Failing to take the needs of the consumer into account would result in a move away from arbitration towards the courts, or a preference for regional arbitration centres that had a track record for rapid resolution, or the more frequent use of other forms of solving disputes. A few years later a Houston-based lawyer observed how many companies were willing to enter into direct negotiation or pursue alternative opportunities rather than be dragged into lengthy arbitration. This is an issue the Institute takes seriously and initiatives are currently underway to help parties analyse exactly what they want from arbitration.

Costs have been a perennial concern but the costs involved in modern arbitration can be staggering. Nael Bunni recalled two recent cases, one involving a claim of nearly $8m that incurred costs of $5m, and another

Arbitrator's Casebook

John Tackaberry QC

An expensive townhouse had been built on an escarpment in South London. The foundations were poor and piles had to be driven deep into the ground. A contractor began excavations for a new project at the foot of the escarpment, ignoring the concerns expressed by the owner of the townhouse. The owner's garden suddenly dropped by six feet and he sued the contractor. The insurer for the owner, John Tackaberry's client, and the insurer for the contractor both happened to be part of the same insurance group. The contractor's insurers paid up as proceedings began but the client's insurers refused to proceed against the contractor's insurers on the grounds they were part of the same group. But John Tackaberry continued with the proceedings, prompting the insurers to make an offer that could not be refused. Rarely does a client recover all his costs and damages; but in this instance the client recovered all his costs and 125 per cent of his damages!

where the claim was £35m, total costs £18m and the final award just £1.5m. In 1995, Dr Michael O'Reilly, recently the Institute's legal advisor but also a qualified engineer and barrister, wrote in the journal how escalating costs were discouraging parties from making valid claims, and advocated the adoption of measures such as costs agreements to bring them under control. Little had changed by 2011 when the Institute noted that in several cases costs had outstripped the value of the dispute. Larger legal teams than necessary, endless submissions by the parties, inflexible and inefficient arbitrators (one tribunal had taken a year to be constituted): all were contributory factors. Emphasizing that costs must be contained if international arbitration was to retain its attraction, the Institute organized a groundbreaking survey of the international arbitration costs. The results showed that nearly two-thirds of costs related to external legal expenses, while

the average case lasted between 17 and 20 months. At the launch of the survey, the legal director of Royal Dutch Shell described international arbitration as 'a rich man's game best left to large companies, insurers and the organs of sovereign states'. Yet again pleas were made for arbitrators to be allowed to devise procedures appropriate and flexible enough for each case. Such measures, it was suggested, could include the limited production of documents, time-limited hearings and the expeditious delivery of awards.

Construction, the major source of domestic arbitration in the UK and elsewhere, was significantly affected by the trend to apply court processes to arbitration. In big construction projects, working on low margins to tight deadlines, time and money were crucial factors. By the mid-1980s the pervasive use in construction arbitration of the adversarial system copied from the courts had already eroded consumer confidence. In the early 1990s a report

Arbitrator's Casebook

Hew Dundas

Hew Dundas served with two local co-arbitrators on a complex case in the Middle East. They worked hard together to craft a single award, integrating the strongly dissenting opinion of one of the arbitrators, and delivered the award on day 56 of a 60-day timescale, with the chairman agreeing the final corrections from the car park of Disneyland, Florida.

Hew Dundas (left).

Annual dinner at Drapers' Hall, London.

on construction arbitration in Australia concluded that the system had 'broken down as a cheap and efficient means of resolving construction disputes'. In some countries, including England and Wales, the result was a move away from arbitration to statutory adjudication.

Yet there is still a future for domestic arbitration, even as it faces competition in many countries from the courts and from alternative forms of dispute resolution. Although it still suffers from the fact that, in Doug Jones's words, 'lawyers conduct arbitration as they would conduct court cases', it still has advantages in jurisdictions where courts are partial, lack independence or display a bias against commerce. In the UK, for instance, its renewed popularity is in reaction to an increasingly costly, underfunded and inefficient court system. It is also being extended into new areas, such as family law, where the merits of speed, cost and confidentiality appeal to the parties involved. Internationally, arbitration still has enormous potential. Many cases proceed without problems, with the full cooperation of lawyers on both sides, resulting in speedy, fair and cost-effective decisions. The continuing attraction

Michael Stephens, President in 2014.

Arbitrator's Casebook

Christopher Ojo

'My toughest case was one in which I was a counsel in an international commercial dispute between a calculating and dubious company and an unsuspecting financial institution which involved a claim of over two billion dollars. I was retained by the financial institution. The proceedings on jurisdiction alone were so protracted that it was like conducting the case on the merits. There was so much discovery as my opponents went on a fishing expedition which was surprisingly permitted by the tribunal. Jurisdiction alone took almost two years to conclude. Don't ask me how long the case on the merits took because there is an adage in my country that "if you use ten years to prepare for madness, how long do you want to rave?"'

of arbitration was evident after the collapse of Communism in Eastern Europe when many newly independent countries passed arbitration laws as an incentive to international trade. More recently campaigns have been initiated in many Asian countries to encourage the greater use of arbitration, partly through lack of faith in the courts, partly because of the inherent advantages of the system. The widespread adoption or adaptation of the Model Law, and the protection given to the enforcement of international awards by the New York Convention, despite lack of uniformity between jurisdictions, has, for example, given confidence to international banking consortia entering into bilateral financial treaties. For large organizations operating across several jurisdictions, arbitration still remains an attractive option.

When the Institute's Patron, Karl-Heinz Böckstiegel, spoke at the Institute's conference in Malaysia in 2008, he

Arbitrator's Casebook

Neville Tait

'It started off so well as an appointment by agreement in a construction arbitration. Three years, 79 letters, two security for costs applications, 15 orders for directions, four changes of solicitor by the claimant, a twice-postponed hearing and a mediation later, I issued an agreed award dismissing the claim and counter-claim. … Throughout I had felt that the claimant's case had some merit and did my best to keep the arbitration alive. With hindsight, it would probably have been to the claimant's financial benefit if I had dismissed the claim in year one for failure to provide security for costs.'

New York branch event, 2013.

foresaw no lessening of the demand for international arbitration. It was being applied to new areas all the time, and he cited the examples of technology, intellectual property and sport. He predicted 'a growing harmonization between national arbitration laws'. As arbitration became global, parties were already selecting arbitrators from any region of the world considered to be the best equipped to deal with a particular dispute. Today London accounts for some 40 per cent of all international arbitration cases, with the next most important centres, New York and Paris, having some 15 per cent each. Singapore is among the fastest growing centres of international arbitration, with the government subsidizing arbitration services, which it sees as an encouragement to inward investment. In 2014 another international centre will be added to the list with the opening of one in Istanbul.

The availability of a pool of appropriately qualified, knowledgeable and experienced arbitrators remains central to the future success of domestic and international arbitration. This has been the constant objective of the Chartered Institute. The Institute began appointing arbitrators in 1925, introduced panels in 1977 and more

Arbitrator's Casebook

Captain Sliva Michael

Captain Michael, a member of the Institute, and an insurance and legal manager at a major fleet operator, found himself negotiating personally with Somali pirates for the release of two captured vessels. A car-carrier and a chemical tanker had been seized by the pirates over Christmas and New Year 2009 in the Indian Ocean off the Gulf of Aden. The crews were held at gunpoint. The initial negotiations lasted six weeks without any movement being made, leading to Captain Michael taking sole responsibility for direct negotiations. It was not a task he relished, given that lives were at stake, and he was subjected to personal intimidation from the pirates. The situation was resolved only after five months. The breakthrough came suddenly, with ransoms agreed for each ship, subject to the safe release of each crew. This happened only after a precisely planned operation to take out the ransom money and release the ships. It was a stressful period for Captain Michael, who took a well-deserved holiday afterwards.

Practical Experience in Maritime Arbitration

Cedric Barclay, *Arbitration*, 1983

Barclay was once invited to act as sole arbitrator in a hearing expected to last no longer than 14 days. In fact, he was one of three involved in a case that endured 134 days over two and a half years. With an aggregate age of 215 years, the three arbitrators had to be insured to cover the costs of an abortive hearing should any one of them die before an award had been made. Old age was not the only risk. The three men found themselves being winched deep inside an ultra-large oil tanker in a rickety wooden cage. At one point they were even threatened with murder. 'Such threats', Barclay wrote, 'are not to be taken lightly. It is so easy to trip a man off the quay at low tide, or while the ship may be ranging at Barons Wharf, and it is only accidentally and unpremeditated to hold his hand against a superheated steam pipe, whose lagging has peeled off at a convenient elbow.'

recently extended appointments to cover all recognized methods of dispute resolution, for which skills learned in arbitration are equally applicable.

The success of any arbitration depends largely on the skills and personal qualities of the arbitrator, who treads a path fraught with hazards and can still be challenged on the grounds of misconduct. Today's arbitrator will usually have dual qualifications, one legal, almost essential today, the other relevant to the case in hand. The burden of responsibility can be great. One Institute member recalled being appointed as sole arbitrator for a case worth nearly a billion dollars and being faced on his first day with an array of nearly two dozen people representing the parties. Empathy, understanding and self-discipline are essential, critical for winning the trust of the parties, for keeping a grasp on the case as it proceeds and for creating a coherent and satisfactory award. John Campbell recalled the example of Cedric Barclay, who would convene a case and then take everyone out to lunch to help them understand his approach and to put them at their ease in discussing the

issues, reconvening the next day. Arbitrators have to work hard not only to be fair, to do justice and to minimize costs, but also to ensure that they are perceived as fulfilling all those responsibilities, for the losing party must always feel that he or she has had a fair hearing and remain favourably inclined towards arbitration. For those with the requisite qualities, the role of arbitrator is a challenging and satisfying career. In the words of Mark Entwistle, after 35 years in practice, 'I love being an arbitrator, it engages me, it's a stimulating experience. Every case is different. There's no question of getting bored'. Margaret Rutherford QC, the first woman to chair the Institute, reflected that 'All my cases gave me great satisfaction: to unravel two contradictory stories, to weigh up all the evidence and to arrive at a carefully considered decision, based on the balance of probabilities and preponderance of evidence, is singularly gratifying'. With the increasing complexity of international commerce, skilled professional arbitrators remain as much in demand as they did in the 1920s, and the Institute's role in providing them remains even more important.

9

ADR – CONCILIATION, MEDIATION AND OTHER FORMS OF DISPUTE RESOLUTION

Other forms of dispute resolution became more popular as a reaction to the perceived disadvantages of formal arbitration. Many of these had distant roots while others were of more recent origin. Conciliation and mediation were probably the most widely practised after arbitration. While most of these alternatives sought to overcome the weaknesses of arbitration, few of them had the advantage of arbitration's legal certainty or its uniform international standards. Although the Chartered Institute took time to embrace these different methods, it has become a respected advocate for mediation in particular, developing a comprehensive education and training programme.

Professor Frank E. A. Sander at Harvard. Sander coined the term Alternative Dispute Resolution (ADR).

Alternative Dispute Resolution (ADR) was first coined as a term by Professor Frank E. A. Sander, an American academic, in 1976. The first address on the subject in the UK was given by Jonathan B. Marks from the US to the Institute conference in 1983. For most practitioners, the definition embraces every alternative to litigation, but for others it excludes arbitration. In the US, for example, ADR does not include arbitration on the grounds that the latter, by virtue of its binding nature, is a distinct process. Arbitration, perhaps the single most important part of ADR, has been discussed in an earlier chapter, and this chapter concentrates on other methods of dispute resolution, notably conciliation and mediation.

Like arbitration, other methods of resolving disputes have been around since time immemorial. In the words of arbitration's leading historian, Professor Derek Roebuck, 'mediation existed before there was litigation of any kind whose excesses it could ameliorate'. There is evidence of mediation being used in what is now modern Syria

Sixth Mediation Symposium, 2013: 'Mediators: Fit for Purpose?'

in 1800 BC. In Asia the Confucian tradition favoured solving disputes through persuasion and agreement, while Buddhism encouraged compromise and litigation was seen as a last resort. This tradition led to an enduring preference for conciliation that still exists today. In many African communities mediation was the common way of addressing disputes, while both mediation and conciliation were embedded in many Islamic cultures. These alternatives were also taken up in the West where Christian clergy were often called upon to act as mediators. In the US mediation was practised by the Quakers, the Jews and the Chinese.

It was during the nineteenth century that mediation and conciliation began to be more widely taken up in the West. These processes were first applied in a major way to disputes between workers and employers. In England the 1896 Conciliation Act laid the foundation for an organization, the Advisory, Conciliation and Arbitration Service (ACAS), which still operates today. In the US conciliation commissioners were appointed for the same purpose in 1913, leading ultimately to the creation of the Federal Mediation and Conciliation Service. Conciliation courts had long been established in Denmark, and their example was advocated in England during the 1920s by one judge who commented that when 'we complacently regard litigation as the only way of settling disputes, our conversation verges on senility'. Strikingly, conciliation was the preferred method for most disputes referred to the ICC before 1939.

The use of conciliation declined after 1945 as the growth of international trade and the complexity of contracts favoured arbitration. By 1988 conciliation accounted for only five per cent of cases dealt with by the

Professor Pieter Sanders.

ICC. Conversely, by then arbitration was under challenge, with rising concern that it was beginning to ape the courts in its procedures, that its proceedings were too often dominated by counsel and that it was becoming more inflexible. Its advantages in terms of speed and cost over litigation seemed in danger of becoming marginal.

This trend, as we have seen, was already exercising members of the Institute. As early as 1975 the Institute's conference discussed the possibility that conciliation should be used as a preliminary or an alternative to arbitration. The Institute introduced facilities for conciliation in 1978 at a time when it had been little heard of in international commercial circles outside the US. A paper delivered to the 1979 conference by Dr Johannes Trappe suggested that arbitrators should have the power to offer conciliation instead of arbitration. But with arbitration still dominant inside and outside the UK, members were slow to take much interest in alternatives.

But conciliation as an option was gaining ground internationally. In 1980, just four years after the Model Rules on arbitration had been agreed, UNCITRAL finalized

Model Rules on conciliation. This gave a major boost to the use of conciliation in international commerce. This was the case even in the US, where the burgeoning costs of litigation had led to entrepreneurial lawyers popularizing conciliation alongside other forms of dispute resolution. The Rules were based on the principles of the complete freedom of the parties, the active assistance of an impartial conciliator, a simple, informal and confidential procedure and a clear separation from adversarial proceedings. The latter principle was important since it enabled the parties to preserve their personal relationship, a quality that was attractive for international businessmen frequently doing business with each other.

In 1981 Professor Pieter Sanders, in an article in *Arbitration* highlighting this development, pointed to the greater use of conciliation and observed how it was preferred to arbitration in China, still one of the world's great untapped markets. Conciliation was also becoming popular in Australia as a preliminary to arbitration, although some suggested that the process was open to abuse, entered into only half-heartedly as a delaying tactic prior to arbitration. The process did have other disadvantages. It was prone to error, unfairness (lack of impartiality on the part of the conciliator) and difficulties in drawing up settlements. For success, it required conciliators of very high reputation and standards and an understanding by the parties of their legal positions. While conciliation was certainly a less complex and less expensive route towards dispute resolution, an article in *Arbitration* in 1990 neatly summed up how it differed from arbitration: 'Conciliators do not make binding awards and so do not exercise a judicial function. The principles of natural justice do not apply. Conciliation operates outside the law. There are no rules of conciliation or procedural imperatives. Conciliators may proceed in any way they please.' In the UK it was still little used, largely because it was unpopular with the legal profession.

In 1989 ADR was the subject of the Institute's annual conference, and in the same year a sub-committee was formed under Tony Canham to develop guidelines for conciliation and mediation. By that time, however, the Institute had already lost the opportunity to take the leading role in forms of dispute resolution other than arbitration.

By this time conciliation was fairly well established in the US, and the subject of serious interest in the UK for the first time, but it was a concept still held in little regard in many civil law countries. Discussing the topic at a meeting of the Institute's European branch in 1994, Professor Sanders pointed out that while many civil law countries had revised their laws on arbitration in recent years, none had taken the opportunity to add provisions governing conciliation. This contrasted with a number of common law countries, such as Bermuda, whose International Conciliation and Arbitration Act, 1994, regulated conciliation in detail and took into account its relationship with arbitration. The reason for such a lukewarm approach to conciliation in civil law jurisdictions was suggested at the same meeting by another speaker, Otto de Witt Wijnen. First, arbitration and litigation had not yet become subject to the excesses in many civil law countries – 'we are not victimized in this part of the world by such horrors as discovery of documents, long protracted hearings and jury trials'. Second, he alleged, business people and lawyers largely settled their disputes in a friendly atmosphere often inconceivable in, for instance, the US. As a French

Institute annual dinner. Guests include Geoffrey Beresford Hartwell (second from left) and Lord Mustill (seventh from left).

colleague had told the speaker, 'Mediation is lunch and we love to lunch'.

Nevertheless, throughout the 1990s the Institute's sub-committee continued its work, in which Nael Bunni was particularly influential. In 1999 one of the modifications made to the Royal Charter granted the Institute the power to extend its activities to forms of dispute resolution other than arbitration. In 2001 the Institute began delivering courses on adjudication and mediation. In 2002, following on from the Model Rules of 1980, the UNCITRAL Model Law on International Commercial Conciliation was adopted. A review of conciliations conducted in the UK concluded in 2005 that nearly three-quarters of them proved successful in reducing disagreements between the parties and producing settlements regarded by the parties as satisfactory.

During the 1980s conciliation had been seen as a helpful intermediate step in seeking a resolution in construction disputes, with experienced arbitrators acting as conciliators. The construction sector appreciated conciliation's major advantage, which was the possibility of securing agreement between the parties on acceptable terms, an attribute eminently suited to occasions where contracts already underway required minor adjustments. In South Africa construction arbitration included conciliation procedures in standard contracts as a precondition for settling disputes prior to seeking arbitration or litigation. In Hong Kong mediation was actively promoted within construction. The UK industry lagged behind, with a limited pool of practitioners with knowledge and experience of dispute resolution processes other than arbitration, but it was expected that a similar approach would soon be adopted.

By the late 1980s, although construction still dominated the workload of domestic arbitrators in England and Wales, the UK construction industry was already starting to change its approach to arbitration. The editorial in the Institute's journal in May 1984 was prescient, observing that 'arbitration, in the construction field at least, in due course will recede to be replaced by other procedures of dispute

International event in the City of London.

resolution'. One Institute member observed in 1986 that while hardly any construction contracts were completed without a claim, it was also true to say that very few claims ever reached formal arbitration because of the costs and delays involved. This was an unsatisfactory situation for the industry, whether contractors or subcontractors, architects or engineers. Instead the practice of adjudication was adopted but this created legal uncertainty over the status of the adjudicator's decisions, and raised concerns about the impact of adjudication on subcontractors. A review of the industry in 1994 strongly recommended the introduction of statutory adjudication, which the government enshrined

in the Housing Grants, Construction and Regeneration Act in 1996. The Act took effect in 1998, with the result that statutory adjudication replaced arbitration in construction disputes in England and Wales.

In theory adjudication resulted in temporary non-binding resolutions, enabling work to continue with a minimum of delay, since it was originally believed that the parties would revisit them at a later date. In practice, this rapid and cost-effective procedure proved very popular, and the vast majority of initial decisions were ultimately accepted as binding by the losing parties and almost all those cases taken to the courts were upheld. As a result, statutory adjudication steadily killed off the use of arbitration in construction. Few members who practised construction arbitration in England and Wales realized the impact statutory adjudication would have, although Harold Crowter, the Institute's Chairman in 1998–9, predicted a steady decline in the use of arbitration. He was right. In 2005 Robert Gaitskell, reviewing trends in dispute resolution, could write in *Arbitration* that statutory adjudication 'now dominates the construction dispute field'. By 2010, arbitration had been reduced by 95 per cent and court cases by half.

Discontent in construction about existing processes for remedying contractual problems was responsible for generating a wide range of new procedures during the late 1990s and early 2000s. This was especially the case in preliminary determination procedures. Adjudication spread steadily initially across many Commonwealth countries, including Australia and Malaysia, and later further afield, for instance into the Middle East, where many major construction projects were undertaken. Other processes that were used included mediation, early neutral evaluation and dispute boards and panels.

Dispute boards in particular became well established. Their origins lay in the concerns of the US construction industry about the rising cost of arbitration and litigation in the 1960s and 1970s. An early example involved the construction of the Boundary Dam in Washington in the

1960s. Dispute boards involved the appointment of a panel of three engineers and/or lawyers at the outset of a project, who would visit the site regularly and deal with incipient disputes, pre-empting the need for arbitration. Complaints were dealt with as they arose and all sides had a hearing. Boards remained in place for the duration of a project and their record was outstanding, with most disputes resolved without the need for arbitration or litigation. The popularity of boards grew steadily after their use on the Eisenhower Tunnel contract in 1975. Dispute boards appealed to contractors engaged on major projects who were concerned about the role of the 'Engineer' as the final arbiter under many contracts and by the early 1980s they were being used internationally. Dispute avoidance has become a major trend in international construction and

many arbitrators have advised parties to take steps at the contract stage to prevent disputes, such as the inclusion of non-confrontational procedures or the requirement for the parties to highlight impending difficulties. Such measures, for instance, were employed for the building of Hong Kong's new airport in 1997 and for the London 2012 Olympics. One of the Institute's most recent initiatives in this field has been the publication of a single set of international dispute board rules in January 2014.

Mediation has probably become the most popular method of dispute resolution other than arbitration. It differs from conciliation in that the mediator does not offer a settlement but simply helps the parties to come together to reach a negotiated settlement between themselves. In the words of one specialist, the mediator is 'a catalyst

Colin Wall and Michael Shand.

resolve business disputes in a business-like manner without recourse to deciding who is right and who is wrong, and while preserving business relationships'.

As with conciliation, mediation became more popular as the apparent disadvantages of traditional arbitration became clear, and it was in the US that the trend first appeared. In 1992 Lord Goff, the Institute's President, noted the debt owed to the US that he described as 'the legal laboratory of the world', for the development of alternatives like mediation. These, he said, were attracting interest around the world, stimulated by the costs, delays, complexity and inflexibility of much modern commercial arbitration. In Australia, for instance, mediation was already commonly used for domestic cases, long before the UK. One Institute member, Mark Mattison, recalled that his first introduction in the UK to mediation came through a lecture in the early 1990s from a visiting Californian professor, who related how the courts in California, in an attempt to reduce congestion, insisted on mediation before a civil case could be listed. It was, said the lecturer, an approach he was certain would be adopted in the UK; in 1999 the use of mediation in the civil courts of England and Wales was formally acknowledged when the courts became

for a resolution designed by the parties'. Sir Michael Kerr observed in 1998 that one of mediation's advantages was that 'usually both sides, instead of only one or neither, come out of the process with a measure of satisfaction'. Colin Wall summed up the process as a way for 'business people to

Mediator's Casebook

Harvinder Singh Bhurji, *The Resolver*, May 2009

'The case concerned an alleged breach of contract arising out of a house extension that had not been completed by the defendant building company as per the contract that had been entered into. The claim was for £94,000. The problem was that the claimant and the defendant were brothers. The opening joint session consisted of hostility coupled with mumbling in Punjabi, which I would not care to translate. This was not going to be one of my smoother mediations.' It turned out that the case dealt with complex family relationships, for which the mediator's understanding of the culture of Asian

families proved essential. After several often tense private sessions with each of the parties, negotiations began, interrupted by a moving speech from the parties' mother, which clearly had an impact on the brothers. An hour later a deal was struck between the brothers, and the solicitors began drafting a mediation agreement. While the brothers refused to resume their own relationship, they were both eager to resolve difficulties with other family members. 'What else could I have done? As mediators we are there to negotiate settlements, not to impose solutions upon them. I can only hope that my intervention has possibly built a way forward for a future relationship to evolve.'

Lord and Lady Goff.

duty-bound to encourage its use in appropriate cases. The practice had also spread to other countries earlier, including South Africa (where it was adopted by the construction industry), Hong Kong and Australia.

By the time the Institute was seeking in vain to obtain the right to award the status of Chartered Mediator in 2005, the practice of mediation was well established in the UK and many other countries worldwide. Although the Institute only organized its first annual mediation symposium in 2008, it was also in this year that it introduced its Fellowship in mediation. The pace of development accelerated, and two years later the Institute issued a Model Mediation Agreement, drawn from the knowledge and expertise of its own members, and sponsored the first UK Mediation Skills Competition. In the same year the Institute published its first guide to ADR. In 2011, as mediation, like arbitration, began to be extended to new areas, the Institute introduced workplace mediation training courses. This was a response to the growing use of mediation around the world, as it became better understood and more sophisticated, thus requiring, as arbitration had done before it, a pool of properly trained and regulated practitioners.

Concerns over the rising cost, delays and complexity of arbitration has led to the development of a whole host of alternative dispute resolution methods since the 1970s. Out of arbitration, conciliation and mediation have emerged options such as early neutral evaluation, Med-Arb (a hybrid between mediation and arbitration) and the mini-trial, many of them emanating from the US.

Of the less widely used alternative methods for resolving disputes, expert determination probably has the longest history. The value of the expert for his or her specialist expertise goes back centuries. It arose first not in the process of expert determination but in the advice of the expert witness. Peter Rees, a previous Chairman of the Board of Management and for several years legal director of Royal Dutch Shell, traced the use of the expert witness to assist the courts back to 1493. The practice is mentioned in the early issues of the Institute's journal and one of the organization's first Presidents, Horace Boot, who held office in 1923–4,

Sir Horace Boot.

Training session at the Cyprus branch.

had extensive experience as an expert witness in important engineering cases. A later President, Bill James, also had an interest in the role of the expert witness, giving lectures to members on the subject during the 1960s and 1970s. His rationale was that the expert witness too was a secondary profession, with practitioners scattered among many different professions and bodies, and he had wanted to see the Institute become a forum for the expert witness as much as the arbitrator. In 1983 the Institute organized a joint conference on the issue with the International Association of Experts. By the 1990s the expert witness was no longer an advocate for the party paying his or her fees but regarded as an advisor to the court or tribunal hearing the case.

The origins of the role of the expert as the judge of a dispute rather than as an advisor are not quite as old. The first reference appears in the decision of an English court in 1754 to throw out an appeal against an expert's determination. The practice originated in the use by the parties of a valuer to make a final judgement on a dispute over a property valuation. Expert determination differs significantly from arbitration: there is no obligation to apply natural justice unless expressly stated; there is no need to give reasons for a decision and the expert can be sued for negligence; and the New York Convention does not apply. But the major attraction of the process lies in submitting essentially technical problems for binding determination on the basis of fact by an expert in the field without recourse to the expense and delay of a legal battle before either an arbitrator or a judge.

Another alternative with more distant roots is Med-Arb, for which there is evidence in the US as early as 1911. The parties are encouraged, usually through a clause in an agreed contract, to pursue a solution through ADR, with the mediator becoming an arbitrator, should mediation fail. The weakness of Med-Arb is that the ultimate arbitral role of the mediator might compromise his or her impartiality during mediation. The mini-trial is of much more recent origin, the first instance taking place in the US in 1977. This was summed up by one speaker at an Institute conference as 'a structured settlement negotiation in which each party's advocate puts his best case to a forum which consists of decision makers from each side with power to settle the dispute and an (optional) neutral party after which the executives meet to endeavour to resolve their differences'. Neil Kaplan had made the point in 1987 that the Chinese had long held that no person was better qualified to conclude an arbitration in the event that conciliation failed than the conciliator. Kaplan noted that the idea had been derided by lawyers for a long time but observed how 'time and experience have taught us that the Chinese may well have a point which is well worth exploring'.

The most recent development has been online dispute resolution (ODR), developed in North America to resolve disputes arising from online transactions. The first decision, relating to the sale of email addresses, was made in 1996. ODR is now being used to settle a wide variety of disputes, its advantages other than speed and reduced costs including the ability to handle disputes at a distance. As time has passed, so judicial enforcement of ODR decisions has also become more common.

Christopher Ojo, a leading member of the Institute in Nigeria, shrewdly observed that the problems besetting arbitration might well come to apply to other forms of dispute resolution:

> ADR has become very fashionable. Indeed, it has come to stay and its use and popularity increase year by year. It is thought that in the near future what is today called alternative dispute resolution may become the main, conventional and predominant method of resolving disputes, thereby making litigation an alternative to ADR.

The role of the expert witness has been a central concern of the Institute.

However, with increased use come sophistication, complication and complexity. If these are not checked or kept within limits, ADR may lose the simplicity and convenience that are its hallmarks.

While there will always be instances when these alternative methods of dispute resolution may be preferable to formal arbitration, the latter still has clear advantages over most of them. Many of these alternatives, like arbitration prior to the New York Convention and the Model Law, lack harmonization worldwide, with standards and procedures differing from jurisdiction to jurisdiction. As Institute member John Redmond wrote in the members' magazine in 2012, 'there is a multitude of dispute resolution processes, all suffering regular and accelerating change, and all varying between countries.' Even in mediation there were huge disparities in practice from one nation to another. As for expert determination, only recently had there been attempts to bring order to a process Redmond described as having been 'a Wild West activity with no rules'. All these processes can also suffer from the same disadvantages as modern arbitration, notably expense and delay. They also have their own inherent weaknesses. Mediation, for instance, is open to abuse by the parties, for example, as a means of discovery or draining one side of funds.

As Redmond observed, 'The search for the Holy Grail of a process that is economic, efficient and reliable will continue indefinitely, because it will never be found, or if it is found, it will not be recognized. Flexibility offers efficiency but appears to be open to abuse. Regulation follows, removing the flexibility and making it more expensive, so we search for another flexible process.' Evidence for this can already be seen in statutory adjudication, which one member interviewed for this book believed was becoming more complex and costly through the growing involvement of the legal profession.

Above all, many of the alternatives to arbitration lack the legal certainty that comes with an enforceable arbitral award, which is the supreme advantage of formal

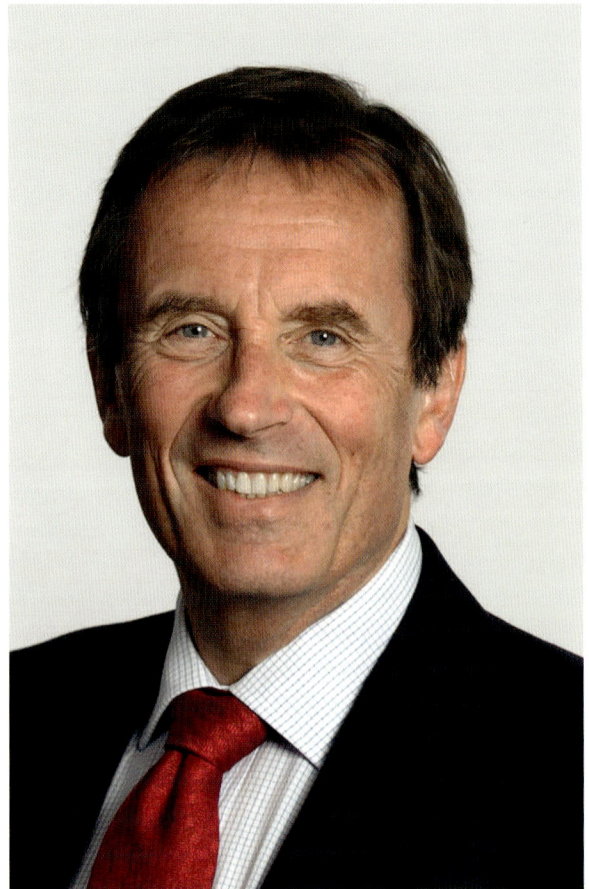

John Redmond.

arbitration. If a non-binding mediation settlement is breached, for instance, the parties often end up in court, creating further delays and expense. For this reason many lawyers would never attempt to use mediation. In an address to a meeting of the Institute in 1998, Professor John Uff had suggested that the alternatives would never supersede arbitration internationally since the prerequisites of mutual consent and understanding and a desire to reach a settlement were usually absent. He was certain that international arbitration, governed as it was by international convention, was 'not only necessary for the proper resolution of international disputes but also forms a significant plank in world order'.

10

EDUCATION AND THE PROFESSIONAL ARBITRATOR

The Institute's principal aim of promoting arbitration and other forms of dispute resolution has always been linked with education, training and the dissemination of knowledge among practitioners. Since the Institute was founded, the journal, Arbitration, *has been the Institute's main method of sharing knowledge. The Institute has also issued its own publications since the late 1920s. While a research arm was discussed at that time, it is only in recent years that this has been properly constituted. Practical education, from mock arbitrations of the 1920s to the wide-ranging courses available today, has been a central part of the Institute's work. In recent years the Institute has developed partnership agreements with several universities around the world.*

From its foundation the Institute aspired to become a learned society. As the Institute's journal put it in 1922, 'study and experience alone constitute the equipment of an Arbitrator'. The journal fulfilled an educational purpose, carrying in-depth articles and analyses of published arbitration cases. The Institute issued its first arbitration guide in 1920, organized occasional meetings of members to discuss learned papers and steadily developed a small library. As a practical way of giving members a better appreciation of managing arbitration cases, mock arbitrations were first held in 1926. These were popular for many years and were soon joined by an annual arbitration team competition.

The Institute's educational work progressed steadily during the late 1920s and throughout the 1930s. This was thanks largely to one member, Alan Davson. In 1927 he pointed out how the American Arbitration Association (AAA), formed only the year before, was already

The Institute's Bloomsbury Square centre has state-of-the-art educational facilities.

collaborating with US law schools and universities and carrying out special studies in conjunction with other bodies. Noting how research had become the driving force behind the AAA, Davson believed the time had come for the Institute to forge ahead with direct services and educational programmes. 'The future of the Institute', said the journal, 'lies in a policy of co-ordination', bringing together accumulated knowledge with a view to becoming recognized as the leading arbitration body.

Davson was instrumental in setting up the Institute's first lecture series that year, linking up with partners like the Westminster Technical Institute, a forerunner of the Recognized Course Provider agreements of recent years. Regular lunches were arranged with guest speakers covering subjects such as 'Psychology in Arbitration'. In 1928 refresher courses were initiated at the Institute's then headquarters in Bedford Square, with further courses

in Birmingham, Bristol, Cardiff and Manchester, the Institute's first activities outside London. In the same year the Institute also published a handbook on procedure and evidence in arbitration.

By 1929, under Davson's chairmanship, an Education Committee had been formed, which began devising a system of examinations. As the speaker at the opening lunch of the 1931 season reminded members, 'The object of the Institute of Arbitrators is to provide a means of justice which is prompt, inexpensive and also efficient by offering to the business community the services of a body of men skilled in various technical branches of industry and commerce, who are also acquainted with the legal incidents of arbitration; and by insisting upon the prompt determination of disputes under the simplest rules of procedure involving small expense'. The Institute looked upon itself to provide such skilled men, particularly as very few bodies included arbitration as part of their own examination syllabuses.

In 1931 examination became the means of entrance for associate members in the belief that an arbitrator must have some grounding in the laws and elements of procedure involved in arbitration. This was not the first hurdle for admission. Any candidate for the associate's diploma was expected to be a specialist in his own field and would not be accepted for the examination without already having obtained qualifications from his or her relevant professional body. The examination covered the law of arbitration, the law of contracts, compulsory purchase (or an option better suited to the candidate's specialism), and procedure and evidence. The candidate with the top marks in the law of arbitration paper would be awarded the Institute prize. The first examination was held in May 1931. It was a groundbreaking event for the Institute and established its reputation for training arbitrators.

Progress was not maintained. As the Institute ran out of energy in the post-war world, its education programme fell into abeyance. Corporate memory was short and the achievements of the interwar years were forgotten. There was no attempt to revise previous publications and by 1952 it fell to members to urge the organization to issue a new guide. Nor was there any attempt to revive the examinations process to set standards of knowledge and skills for arbitrators comparable with standards in other professional bodies.

Renewal began in the 1960s. The long-defunct Education Committee was re-established and evening lectures and discussion meetings were revived. In 1963, with more than a thousand members for the first time, the Institute launched its first new education and training initiative for many years. In March that year Alwyn Waters and Leslie Alexander organized a three-day residential course on arbitration, intended to become an annual event. It was held at the Institute of Advanced Architectural Studies at the newly founded University of York, with members acting as lecturers and tutors.

In 1967 the Institute's annual report recorded how 'the Institute has greatly enlarged its activities in the field of education and it is intended that this should continue. The Council feels that the provision of education and training facilities for members of the Institute, as well as others, is one of the more important aspects of the work of the Institute'. In the following year renewed interest was taken in the Institute's admission standards, with minimum academic attainments agreed by Council. By then, the annual residential courses, regularly oversubscribed, alternated between the universities of York and Bristol, and other courses had been held at places such as Slough College, the Holborn College of Law and the College of Estate Management. Practice arbitrations were proving ever more successful, with one demonstration at Leeds University in 1969 attracting an audience of more than 300 architects, builders and surveyors. Others were beginning to follow the Institute's example, with the UK's first training

The Institute of Advanced Architectural Studies, University of York, venue for the 1963 course on arbitration.

course in arbitration for lawyers held by the British Legal Association in 1970.

In the 1970s Bill James took up the mantle from Alan Davson. In 1972 Cedric Barclay described James as setting 'such a furious pace in furthering our education'. As President in 1970–1, James had pressed for a much broader education and training programme. He wanted one that continued to involve third parties, extended the scope of training beyond construction, and embraced the role of the expert witness and conciliator as well as the arbitrator. He was critical of the Institute's failure to conduct in-depth research into the law and practice of arbitration and to establish adequate research facilities for members. He understood that the quickening pace of international trade and the rising number of arbitrations demanded more qualified arbitrators more quickly, and he was eager for the Institute to fulfil this role.

New members were still being admitted without examination or specific training in arbitration, with the only requirement being appropriate primary professional

Anthony Abrahams discusses membership of the Institute.

qualifications. Under the influence of James, supported by Bertie Vigrass, this began to change as steps were taken for the first time since the 1930s to revive the Institute's examinations. Council agreed to establish a formal structured training programme, and by 1974 there were introductory, intermediate and advanced training courses for practising arbitrators, offered at a variety of locations across the UK. Leslie Alexander and Ray Turner played a prominent role in the early development of these courses. Several colleges and universities were persuaded to include arbitration as part of their diploma or degree courses, which became officially recognized by the Institute. This was a process that continued throughout the 1980s and 1990s.

A knowledge of the law was a strengthened component of the new regime, which Vigrass felt was particularly important for arbitrators in the changed and more complicated commercial world. Rules were also laid down for becoming a Fellow of the Institute. Candidates had to be an existing associate member and pass a second examination. Another requirement was the completion of a period attached to experienced members to gain a practical understanding. In addition, no member would be admitted as a Fellow unless he or she was adjudged after interview to be capable of becoming a member of the Institute's panels of arbitrators, from which arbitrators were appointed when the Institute was specified by the parties as the nominating body. These too were reformed, divided into eight main areas of activity and 38 subcategories, with panel members placed in one of three grades, based on qualifications and experience.

In 1974 J. R. W. Alexander was largely responsible for organizing the Institute's first arbitration conference, held at Fitzwilliam College, Cambridge, and attended by 72 arbitrators, including members from New Zealand and Trinidad. Alexander, a long-serving member, had been the Institute's first President from outside London. He had taken a keen interest in the widest possible promotion of arbitration and had been one of the few members to keep the organization going during the difficult years immediately after the Second World War. In his honour a new lecture series was instituted in November 1974. The inaugural lecture was given by Lord Denning, probably the most famous English judge of his time. It was Denning who in a judgement given in 1952 had come down very firmly on the side of the arbitrator: 'When traders go to lay arbitrators, the matter should be left to the arbitrators without querying their decision on a point of law. If people want to raise a point of law, they ought to ask at the time for a case to be stated. If no such request is made, they should leave the law to the arbitrators'. He had done the same thing in the year he gave his lecture. The Hadjitsakos shipping case involved an arbitral award against the charterers of the vessel, which was referred to the court of appeal on the grounds that the key point was the legal interpretation of the working of the charter party. The court was split over the issue of whether or not arbitrators should judge law as well as fact, with Denning siding with the two arbitrators, unlike his two colleagues, although the award was confirmed by a two-to-one decision.

The next four lectures were given by equally distinguished judges, Lord Diplock, Lord Roskill, Lord Scarman and Lord Mackenzie Stuart. The Alexander Lecture was a showcase for arbitration, helping the Institute

Above and top right: arbitration conference organized by the Institute.

to fulfil its primary aim of promoting the practice as widely as possible. In the following year the Institute also took the first step towards realizing James's vision of expanding the concept of arbitration when the first residential training course covering the role of the expert witness was held at Reading university.

Another initiative taken in the early 1970s was the development of a correspondence course that could be offered internationally. This was the first time that the Institute had extended its educational provision beyond the UK. From small beginnings the Institute developed a more extensive international programme. A leap forward was taken under John Tackaberry's chairmanship, when the Institute's training and education provision was revised once more to take into account more diverse cultures

Presidents

Neil Kaplan

Neil Kaplan is a self-made man of many parts. Neil relishes the intellectual challenge of being an international arbitrator. He is unarguably one of the most in-demand international arbitrators in the world. Neil joined the Institute in 1979 and became a Chartered Arbitrator in 1980.

I first met Neil in the early 1980s when I was part of a delegation of UK members attending the Institute's annual conference, being held that year in Hong Kong. At that time Neil was a leading light at the Hong Kong Bar, where he was very active on diverse cases, including a number of construction disputes – unsurprising given that any observant visitor might have described Hong Kong as the largest building site in the world on the smallest plot of land.

Others know better his career before I met him, and a friend of Neil's has provided the following words to record his recollection of the development in Neil's career both before and in Hong Kong. David Wyld writes:

Neil Kaplan practised at the English Bar from 1965 to 1980. Even as a junior he stood out as an exceptionally able practitioner in work in the Commercial Court, the Chancery Division and in Arbitrations. He showed an ability to grasp facts and law in a diverse range of cases. At the end of 1980 he was invited to join the Attorney General's Chambers in Hong Kong. He started practising in Hong Kong in 1981, in charge of the Civil Litigation Section of the Chambers of the Attorney General, then John Griffiths QC.

He quickly took a firm grip on the conduct of litigation and such was the respect which he quickly gained that he became appointed QC in Hong Kong in 1982.

As well as being in charge of the administrative arrangements in the Civil Litigation Unit, he also regularly appeared for the Hong Kong Government in cases both in Hong Kong and in the Privy Council. He soon gained the respect of the Lords of Appeal in Ordinary as they then were

Neil Kaplan QC then left the employment of the Attorney General's Chambers and set up his own Chambers practising at the Bar in Hong Kong. He quickly established a reputation as one of the top QCs in commercial and administrative matters.

In March 1990 he was appointed a Judge of the Supreme Court of Hong Kong. In addition to his duties in that position, which he held until 1994, he was also responsible for setting up the Hong Kong International Arbitration Centre, and served as its first Chairman from 1991 to 2004. In 1994 he stood down from his position as a Supreme Court Judge (where he gained the reputation as being the safest pair of hands in resolving commercial and administrative disputes) in order to devote more time to running the Arbitration Centre in Hong Kong and sitting as Arbitrator himself.

It is a mark of the respect rightly accorded to his grasp of international arbitration practice that his decision in the High Court of Hong Kong in 1993 in Lucky Gold Star (Hong Kong) Limited vs. Nag Moo Kee Engineering

Limited is recognized as a landmark in International Arbitration practice. He held that where parties, possibly through ignorant or hurried lawyers, had entered into an arbitration agreement in a contract which referred disputes to 'The International Commercial Arbitration Association', court proceedings should be stayed in favour of arbitration despite the fact that no such organization had ever existed. The clear intention of the parties had been that the disputes should be referred to arbitration and effect would be given by the Courts to that intention. This decision is well known and referred to in writings on international arbitration.

I got to know Neil well in that I met him in my later yearly visits to Hong Kong where I would lead a team of Hong Kong members of the Institute in carrying out Institute viva voce workshop assessments of arbitral

knowledge, self-presentation and judgement of Hong Kong and Pacific Rim-based arbitral aspirants seeking election to Fellowship of the Institute. Neil was a fearsome interrogator of those who aspired to pass this challenging oral examination having already successfully passed the Institute's written examinations.

It was the development of my friendship with Neil and my recognition of his standing as an arbitrator of international repute that led me to seek his personal contribution to my wish to raise significantly the international profile of the Institute following an earlier initiative by a fellow Vice President.

Until 1989 there had been a routine and historic progression of Institute Council members to Chairmanship of the Chartered Institute of Arbitrators, with the Chairman being chosen by recent previous holders of that post. This

The Hong Kong Supreme Court, where Neil Kaplan was a judge from 1990 to 1994.

archaic process did not always result in the best choice of Chairman for the Institute, and it was broken by new blood on Council in the late 1980s that led to democratic elections of Vice Presidents, including myself and John Tackaberry QC, who became Chairman in the Jubilee 75th year of the Institute in 1990.

The first positive initiative towards internationalization of the Institute was that of John Tackaberry, who conceived Special Fellowship Courses abroad, including my earlier devised viva voce interrogation assessment of those aspiring to Fellowship in the UK, to encourage foreign lawyers to join the Institute to increase the international membership in the face of static numbers of UK members. The Institute had hitherto been largely a membership of construction industry professionals, maritime professionals and some solicitors.

My later initiative in 1998 was for a major increase in the international profile of the Institute by encouraging more international arbitrators to join the Institute. Council approved my proposal and I arranged a one-year break in the succession arrangements in order to facilitate Neil becoming a Vice President, then Millennium President, in order to promote and communicate properly the international standing of the Institute. Neil at that time was Chairman of the Hong Kong International Arbitration Centre, of which he was a founder in 1985, and a member of the Council of the International Council of Commercial Arbitration (ICCA).

Marketing as a development initiative had the desired effect. The Institute membership has increased progressively by a third since then, now some 12,000 members worldwide, and the number of overseas members of the Institute now exceeds that of the UK membership.

The benefit of the dedicated patronage of Neil Kaplan during the years either side of the Millennium, which continues, has undoubtedly made a significant contribution to the present international standing of the Chartered Institute of Arbitrators.

Neil was awarded a CBE in 2001 for services to International Arbitration and he was awarded an SBS (Silver Bauhinia Star) by the Hong Kong SAR in 2007 to reflect his efforts in promoting HKIAC and Hong Kong as the dispute resolution hub of Asia.

It has been my honour to work with him both in connection with the Chartered Institute of Arbitrators and as a fellow member of international arbitration tribunals.

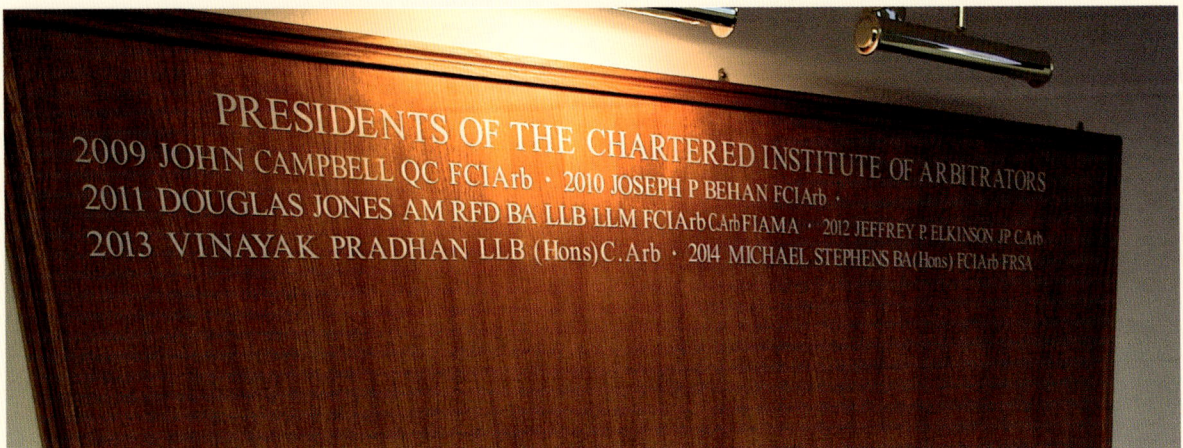

PRESIDENTS OF THE CHARTERED INSTITUTE OF ARBITRATORS

2009 JOHN CAMPBELL QC FCIArb · 2010 JOSEPH P BEHAN FCIArb ·
2011 DOUGLAS JONES AM RFD BA LLB LLM FCIArb CArb FIAMA · 2012 JEFFREY P. ELKINSON JP CArb
2013 VINAYAK PRADHAN LLB (Hons) C.Arb · 2014 MICHAEL STEPHENS BA(Hons) FCIArb FRSA

Brian Eggleston, Tony Canham, Karen Gough and James Leckie.

Anthony Canham

Tony Canham joined the Institute of Arbitrators, as it was then, as an Associate Member in October 1968, membership No. 901. He joined the Institute because, as the second in command of construction on the site of the new Police Training Academy at Hendon, London, he had a difference of opinion with the architect regarding the latter's right to issue an instruction to design and build a complicated precast, post-tensioned concrete support structure for three steel boiler chimneys. He declined to accept the written instruction on the basis that the contractor had no design liability under the contract. A dispute arose. The variation instruction was eventually withdrawn.

Tony realized that in order to become an effective manager of major construction contracts he ought to be able to understand the law on interpretation of contracts. He decided that the best source of education on such matters lay with arbitrators, who routinely decided such issues when lawyers could not reach agreement. Following interview by a panel of three senior arbitrators, chaired by Norman Royce, the most famous UK arbitrator of the time, he was elected a Fellow of the Institute in February 1977.

Tony was then appointed an Institute panel arbitrator in 1977 on the ABTA Consumer Travel Scheme and on National House Building Council contractual arbitrations. He later became National Convenor of the NHBC Panel of Arbitrators. His UK construction industry arbitration work had developed by 1982. He became an International Arbitrator in 2000.

Tony attended and took part in his first Institute Conference in 1977 at St Andrews in Scotland; Walter Jacob was President. Tony was soon after approached by an immediate past President, John Corkill, and past President Cedric Barclay, to become a member of the General Purposes Committee, the equivalent of the current Board of Management. He was elected to Council around 1982 and served on it for more than 20 years, with an intermediate break of three years. He served on many committees, such as the Professional Conduct Committee, and chaired numerous others, including the Chartered Institute of Arbitrators inaugural ADR Committee and the Executive Board. He is currently Chairman of the Professional Conduct Committee.

He was elected as a Vice President of the Chartered Institute of Arbitrators in 1988. As Chairman elect of Council for

Presidents

1990 he forward-planned the 75th-year jubilee of the Institute, However, he decided not to offer himself for annual re-election as Vice President due to other business commitments, which would have limited his availability in the jubilee year. Ronald Bernstein QC and John Tackaberry QC were elected Vice Presidents, and Tony worked with John Tackaberry, on his becoming Chairman elect of the Institute for the jubilee year, with completion of the planning and organization of events for that landmark year.

Tony qualified as a Chartered Civil Engineer and at the age of 32 became the youngest Fellow elected on record. Tony was President of the Society of Construction Arbitrators from 2010 to 2013 and was a member of the three-man Mediation Training team at the Academy of Experts for some ten years. The team's activities included training for Hong Kong Government employees and for the Government of the seven constituent countries in the Caribbean.

In order to raise the international profile of the Institute he personally persuaded Neil Kaplan QC, a past International Vice President, to become President of the Institute in the millennium year.

Growth and Development of Education and Training Internationally

In 1981 Tony and Maurice Pleasance (Chairman of the Institute in 1989) devised, at the request of the then Chairman of Council Gordon Hickmott, a new, largely viva voce-based course to provide assessment of members aspiring to Fellowship with practical experience of procedural problems that only occur in real-life arbitrations. That format was adopted and refined with more emphasis on written questions leading to the currently used scenarios and questions used in the International and Domestic Accelerated Route to Fellowship Modules on which Tony is still currently a regular assessor.

That 1981 assessment and accreditation format was used by Tony in his conceived, Institute-approved, mission to ensure

that candidates for Fellowship of the Institute were assessed in any part of the world in the same format and on the same marking basis to the same standard. As a result all Fellows are accredited at the same level worldwide. That is one of the core factors that led to the Institute being described as having provided 'the Gold Standard' for training in arbitration.

He carried out courses, training and coaching Branch Officers to the adopted international standards of assessment, in Hong Kong, Kenya, Nigeria and North America. In North America the programme was carried out in various regions with law faculties of universities hosting an 'Arbitration Program'. Whilst working in some five different principal USA centres Tony promoted the formation of Institute Chapters as North America was geographically too large to initially support multiple branches. He also ran the Assessment Courses in Ireland, the Channel Islands, in Zimbabwe and preceding International American Bar Association Conferences. He participated in a range of Institute courses in Bermuda, Thailand and Egypt.

Dispute Resolution Services

In 2006 the Institute decided to form a wholly owned limited company, IDRS, to carry out the management and control of its Consumer Redress activities that had formerly been carried out within the charity.

The legal importance of the independence of that company, from the charitable activities of the Institute, was recognized by the Trustees, and Tony was identified as a person who could ensure that independence. He accepted the role of a director and was elected Chairman of the Board of Directors by his fellow non-executive directors. He oversaw the development and market adaptation of the company with his fellow directors, in challenging commercial times, for a period of five years until the Trustees approved the sale of the company, as a going concern, to another charity.

An Arbitrator's Career

Neville Tait

Neville Tait qualified as a civil engineer. He first became involved with arbitration as a construction contracts manager. He joined the Institute in 1980, became a Fellow in 1984 and gained his first appointment as an arbitrator in 1988. Since then he has had experience of more than 500 cases. He has also acted as a mediator, conciliator, adjudicator and expert witness. He established his own consultancy in 1995. His first referral came out of the blue, probably because the parties involved appreciated his civil engineering expertise, but it was a further two years before he was appointed to another case. Progress came through knowledge, experience and reputation combined with networking and raising his profile.

The Institute delivered its first course in Seoul in 2010.

and different traditions in the various jurisdictions where Institute members were found around the world. As a result, by the late 1990s the Institute was offering 69 courses in 19 different jurisdictions, including an international entry course and international diploma. This continues to expand: in November 2010, for instance, the Institute delivered its first course in Seoul in South Korea.

As well as reaching out to international members, the Institute was trying to reach potential members in different professions. In particular, given the up-and-down relationship there had been between members who were lawyers and those who were not, serious efforts were made to strengthen ties with the legal profession. In the early 1990s, during Margaret Rutherford's time as chair, the Institute's engagement with the legal profession had led the College of Law to include arbitration as an optional subject for its Legal Practice Course. At the end of the decade, another chair, Harold Crowter, attacked 'lawyer bashing' and worked instead to establish stronger relationships with the Bar and the Law Society. He believed that the more lawyers knew about arbitration, the better it would be for the profession and the Institute, and he continued to encourage universities to include arbitration as part of their

law syllabuses. His successor, Neil Kaplan, the first of the new-style Presidents, sustained the theme, believing that the more lawyers who joined the Institute, the more they would appreciate the virtues of arbitration. At the time just over a fifth of English members and just less than two fifths of international members were lawyers.

As the Institute's educational approach became more sophisticated, admission to membership became defined by formal 'pathways', including examinations. Links with

An Arbitrator's Career

Mark Entwistle

Mark Entwistle qualified as a quantity surveyor and as a barrister in order to further his career in arbitration. For him, 'Membership [of the Institute] is the gold standard for domestic arbitration and jurisdictions around the world.' He appreciated that for many budding practitioners the conundrum was that membership of an appointments panel required experience, but without experience it was difficult to join a panel.

colleges and universities were formalized with their approval by the Institute as Recognised Course Providers (RCPs). This too embraced an international dimension, with RCPs including the universities of Dublin, Hong Kong, Salamanca and San Pablo. Students taking accredited courses, whose standards were rigorously monitored by the Institute, were exempted from the Institute's own admissions procedures. At the same time, tied in with the aim of promoting arbitration, training courses are still held for interested non-members.

In recent years, beginning under Michael Forbes Smith, the Institute has realized a long-held ambition to develop its own research arm. In 2008 the research team made a valuable contribution to the review of civil litigation costs in the English courts. An intern scheme was established to help institute and develop research projects. This has become highly regarded, attracting high-calibre research students from leading universities, who are helped to publish articles in leading scholarly journals. The Institute's own research staff also publish articles, cementing the organization's growing reputation. Recently a decision by the Maltese Supreme Court cited an article from the journal, surely the supreme accolade for an intellectual journal. The journal has succeeded in filling a particular niche by presenting a peer-reviewed practitioner's point of

Graduates from the Leeds Metropolitan MSc in Construction. Lord Mustill is in the middle of the back row.

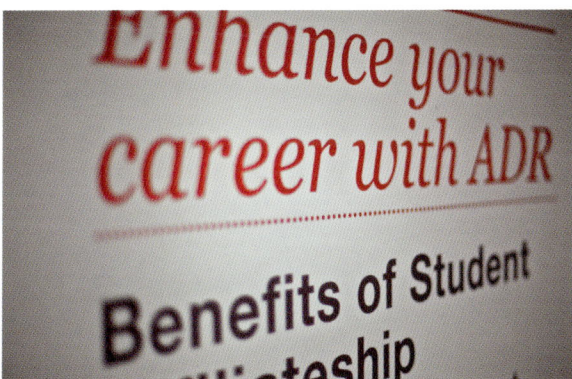

Left: the Institute's Bloomsbury Square premises, centre of learning and innovation.

view on diverse issues. The research department has also expanded the Institute's long tradition of issuing its own publications. Since the late 1990s many of them have been translated into several languages, acknowledging not only the diversity of the Institute's membership, but also that resolution of international disputes involves a multitude of different languages. The series of practice guidelines developed by the Institute's standards committee are regarded as exceptional within arbitration and have also helped to raise the organization's profile.

The status of Fellow and of Chartered Arbitrator are highly regarded worldwide and in 2012 the Institute held its first graduation ceremony for Fellows. This was a great success, attended by 70 of the 250 members from around the world who qualified as Fellows that year. The sum total of all this is that the Institute, in the words of one Past President, has become 'the world's premier arbitral training body'.

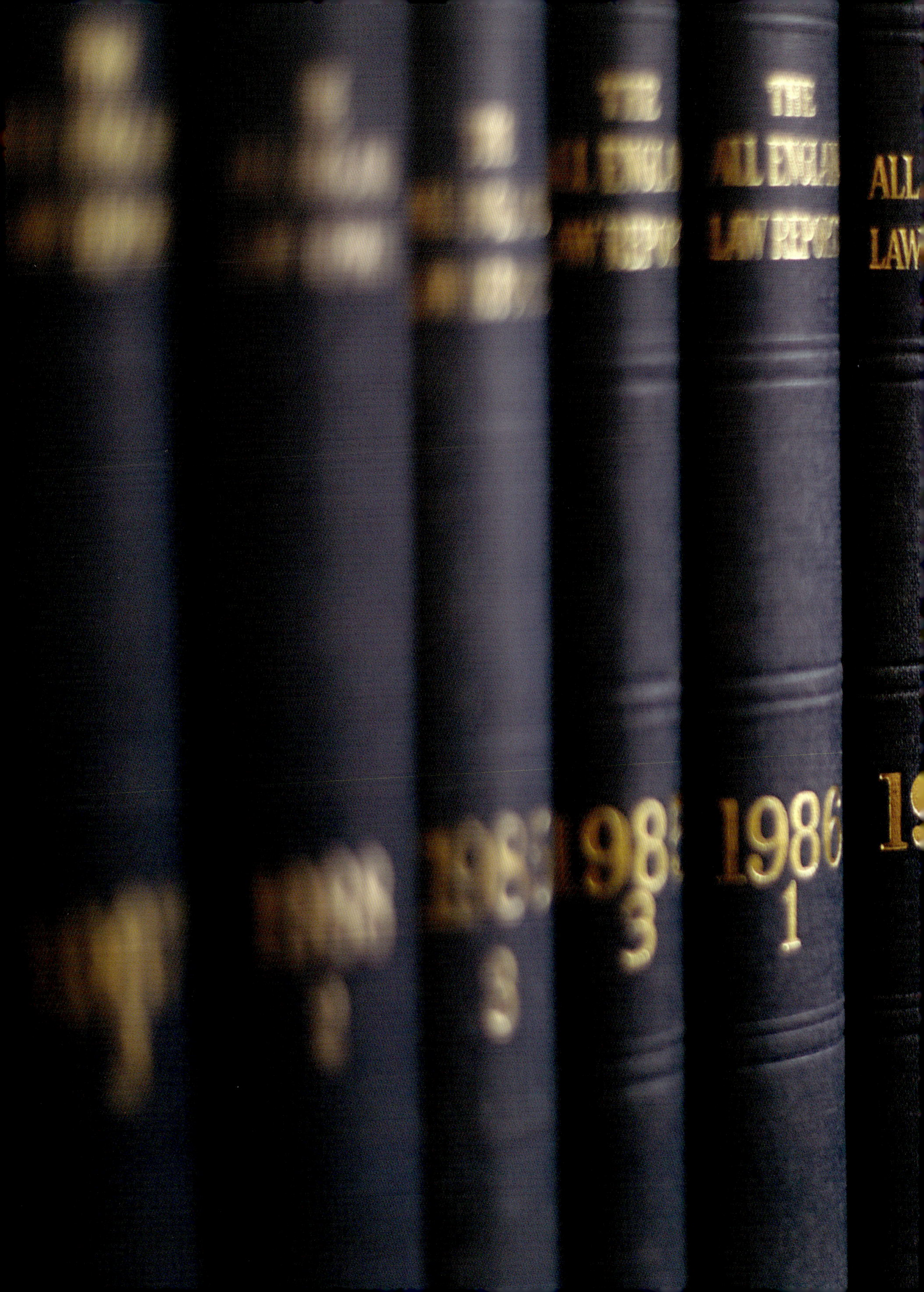
THE
1986
1
3

Part 4

THE CHARTERED INSTITUTE
OF ARBITRATORS AT 100

11

HELPING DISPUTE RESOLVERS AROUND THE WORLD

As the only international membership body for the profession, the Institute is taking a global role in shaping dispute resolution. This is met partly through the Institute's responsibilities as a learned society, developing policy and research, spreading best practice, advising governments and other bodies and collaborating with similar organizations to harmonize global standards.

The Institute has made great strides since the beginning of the new millennium. Its membership was continuing to grow, its methods of governance had become more effective and more representative, it was developing a

India branch members enjoy an event.

reputation for considered and relevant research, its links with other education providers were being deepened while its own provision grew stronger, and it was embracing alternative dispute resolution in the broadest sense. All these factors combined to elevate the Institute's worldwide profile.

The Institute's influence in the world of dispute resolution stems from the strength of its international composition and organization. When the Greek government was preparing for the implementation of the European Union mediation directive, it was the Institute to which it turned on the basis of its global presence and reputation, and the first group of mediators was accredited in 2008. Under Michael Forbes Smith as Director General, membership grew at more than two per cent per annum and by 2012 exceeded 12,000 people. Six more branches (Bahamas, Caribbean, India, Mauritius, Singapore and South Africa) and 22 more chapters were formed, taking the Institute to 68 branches and chapters in 37 countries, with members spread across 110 countries. There were further improvements in communications with international members. The Institute took full advantage

International Diploma course at Keble College, Oxford. Jeffrey Elkinson is in the second row, third from right.

of the digital revolution, initiating a monthly electronic magazine, *The Resolver*, emailed to every member. Efforts were being made to attract younger members, and the Young Members Group, formed in 2011, held its inaugural conference in Dublin in 2012, under chairman Gonçalo Malheiro from Portugal.

The Institute's financial base became more secure. With the support of Malcolm McMullan and his successor, Clare Hughes, as Director of Finance, central costs were reduced, income increased, largely through room hire, and the opportunity was taken in 2011 to acquire the freehold of the neighbouring property, 14 Bloomsbury Square, which the Institute already leased. In the same year the Institute had disposed of its commercial arm, IDRS, which administered more than a hundred arbitration, adjudication and mediation schemes, but whose activities had been hit by the recession.

In 2012 Anthony Abrahams succeeded Michael Forbes Smith as Director General. A qualified solicitor specializing in civil litigation, he came with extensive experience of legal practice management and sat as a deputy district judge. He had also attained the rank of colonel in the Territorial Army, serving in Iraq in 2006 in the Office of the Staff Judge Advocate.

He inherited a strategy, revised following the successful implementation of the groundbreaking Agenda for Change, with four clear themes in which the common factor was the Institute's members. The first recognized that it was only this worldwide resource that gave the Institute the stature that made it a respected and influential force in

Singapore members' evening, 2014.

dispute resolution. This placed it in the position of being able to collaborate with similar bodies worldwide in sharing best practice and in expanding the global reach of dispute resolution, backed up by policy development and research. The other three themes took into account that to sustain this influence, and as more members joined the Institute, this resource had to be nurtured. The Institute was, after all, a membership organization. So the second emphasized the importance of high professional skills and standards, secured through the provision of an education and training programme flexible enough to meet the needs of members, their first professions, specializations, cultures and jurisdictions. Further improving links with branches and chapters was the substance of the third theme, reinforced by the fourth, which also focused on delivering excellence

to the members and others linked with the Institute.

These themes have been developed further under the new Director General. The international aspect of the Institute carries on growing. In the year Abrahams took over, a Korean chapter was formed in Seoul and a new Zambia branch was established in Lusaka. In Europe membership was growing at 15 per cent a year, giving the branch 500 members and leading to the election of the first trustee representing mainland Europe, Axel Reeg. He himself believed this was another step towards bringing common law and civil law closer together. By the end of 2012, after further changes in representation, the Board of Trustees comprised five trustees elected by UK members and seven from outside the UK. As the Institute entered 2014, it had 12,750 members and 37 branches (following the founding of the New York branch), with 64 per cent of members outside the UK, and East Asia its largest branch.

With courses offered in 32 countries and a thousand practitioners being trained every year, there was a need to ensure consistently high global standards. A review of the way the Institute delivered training concluded there should be a greater emphasis on sharing best practice worldwide. In 2013 this led to a London conference for trainers from branches all over the world. The Institute's education and training programme attracts a widespread clientele and receives consistently high satisfaction ratings from participants. Part of this satisfaction comes from the fact that the Institute's courses are largely designed by practitioners to be of value not only to arbitrators, mediators and adjudicators, but also to those who act on

behalf of the parties involved in disputes. As an example of the scope of the Institute's training activities, the Europe branch offered more than 20 courses in ten different locations in 2013, and in 2014 this increased to more than 30 courses. Such high quality programmes, under a body of highly qualified and committed tutors, examiners and assessors, is a great attraction to potential members.

The Institute's connections with leading academic bodies stretch ever further around the globe, from Oxford and Salamanca to Harvard and the Institute of European Studies. The agreement with the University of Salamanca was an initiative aimed at practising lawyers, judges and other officials wherever Spanish was spoken worldwide. As such, it gave the Institute the opportunity to break new ground in areas where its influence was thinly spread,

Sixth Mediation Symposium, 2013.

such as Latin America, where the concept of ADR itself was just beginning to grow. When Vinayak Pradhan became President in 2013, he was also eager to see the Institute 'opening branches in nations where English is not the mother tongue but is increasingly used as the definitive language in international commercial contracts. While India and China are obvious examples, countries like Burma, Cambodia, Laos, Vietnam, Mongolia and South Korea also come to mind'. The Institute's advice was increasingly sought by governments, such as Nepal and Vietnam, and other organizations in many different countries. Other initiatives have included the organization of the first ever international arbitration workshops and award-writing examination to be held in Brazil, which took place in São Paulo in conjunction with the Committee for Brazilian Arbitration and the Committee for Arbitration and Mediation of the Brazil-Canada Chamber of Commerce; and an agreement with the International Centre for Education in Islamic Finance for the inclusion of arbitration as a teaching module. At the same time effort has been redoubled in fostering the Institute's principal

aim, with the strengthening of the Institute's marketing staff for the more effective promotion of non-court dispute resolution worldwide. In November 2013 the Institute also arranged the first annual invitation-only Dispute Appointment Service convention to debate the future of ADR, covering international arbitration, mediation and adjudication. The main speaker, Lord Justice Jackson, author of the report into the costs of civil litigation in the UK, took as his theme an issue of current concern in the field of arbitration, the need for cost-efficient and cost-effective case management.

But the Institute also remains concerned to promote domestic arbitration. One innovation has shown a way forward. A local arbitration scheme was launched in 2009 in the Yorkshire region in the UK as a way of resolving business-to-business and technical disputes through a simple, expedient and inexpensive procedure, administered by the local branch of the Institute. In Scotland the Northern Chapter of the Scottish Branch has been raising awareness of ADR among the North Sea oil and gas sector. This was a long-term campaign, originating in 2009, when a

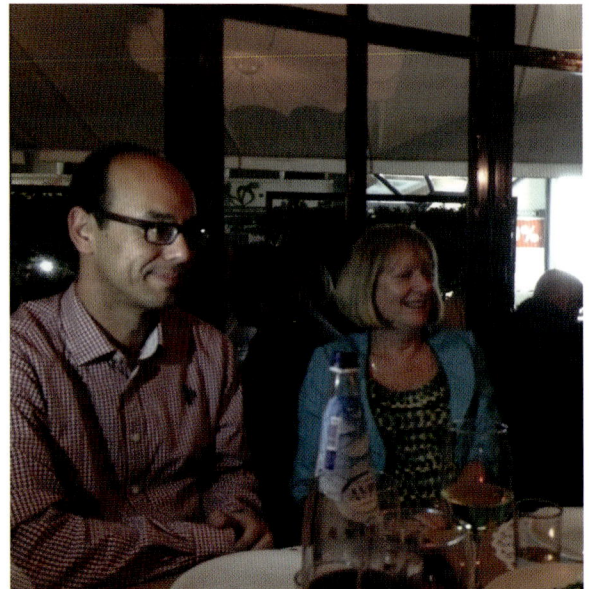

Cyprus branch annual cocktail reception, 2013.

presentation made by a senior Shell executive revealed how the major oil companies were striving to settle differences between themselves without going to court or using arbitration, which they perceived to be a slow process. The Chapter had taken the view that new legislation in Scotland (the Arbitration (Scotland) Act, 2010) would make arbitration much more attractive, especially when costs in Scotland were compared with those in, for instance, London, which was where most of the cases between oil companies were held. Forging links with the Scottish government, and involving the new Scottish Arbitration Centre, part-funded by the Scottish Branch, the Chapter helped to launch the International Centre for Energy Arbitration in association with the Centre for Energy, Petroleum and Mineral Law and Policy at Dundee university. By 2013 this and other measures had seen steady progress in persuading the sector to regard ADR and its advantages more seriously.

As for nurturing the Institute's principal resource, its members, the Institute is investing in the younger generation, taking on board the plea from one younger

Anthony Abrahams addressing the New York branch, 2013.

India branch event in Mumbai.

member, Artem Doudko, at the Dublin conference, that the Institute should organize specific training courses and assist in appointing them as arbitrators or putting their names forward for appointment whenever possible. Achieving appointments following the appropriate qualification, whether in arbitration, mediation or adjudication, has been a common concern among many members. The problem is that chartered status can be achieved only with experience, yet opportunities for such experience have become fewer. Since arbitration will only ever be a second profession, the Institute has to work hard to ensure that its qualifications remain indispensable to members. The Presidential Panels have been more active in making appointments (in under two years these multiplied almost tenfold), and this led to an initiative to further expand the market by identifying ADR clients in international and domestic markets and making the Institute's headquarters available for hearing cases. The Dispute Appointment Service, set up in 2012 and headed by Waj Khan, oversaw 125 appointments in its first year.

In the UK the difficulty in finding appointments was partly historic, stemming from a misplaced belief in some quarters, dating back decades, that the Institute's remit was confined solely to construction. This was a myth Anthony Abrahams hoped to dispel, and the attendance of distinguished leading UK practitioners at the centenary conference in London indicates the progress being made. In addition, to help UK members, the Institute established the Property Disputes Service in 2014 offering alternatives to court for disputes between landlord and tenant, over issues such as easements and rights of way, property ownership and interference, and creating panels of suitably qualified practitioners to act as property dispute resolvers.

The Institute was also aware that very few members were female. Although this was partly historical, the Institute felt a responsibility to begin redressing the balance. In 2012, of 12,501 members, women accounted for 1,809, or 14 per cent. In fact, this position showed a steady improvement from a decade previously when less than seven per cent of members were female. In 2013, as part of the process of welcoming the participation of more women

Professor Dr Karl-Heinz Böckstiegel.

in its affairs, the Institute organized its first workshop to celebrate International Women's Day. With the theme of 'Women as catalysts for change in conflicts justified by religious belief', this successful event attracted 70 people.

On 1 January 2014 the Institute appointed its fourth patron. The list was an illustrious one. The first patron was the Honourable Mrs Anson Chan in 2005–7, who had been the Chief Secretary for Administration in Hong Kong, that is, the head of the civil service. Her successor had been Professor Dr Karl-Heinz Böckstiegel, the leading international arbitrator, in 2008–10, followed by the distinguished judge Lord Phillips of Worth Matravers, founding President of the Supreme Court of England and Wales, in 2011–13. The patron overseeing the celebration of the Institute's centenary is Chief Justice Sundaresh Menon of Singapore. He is highly regarded among fellow practitioners in arbitration. Colin Wall, a leading arbitrator, long-standing member and former President, reflecting

The Honourable Mrs Anson Chan.

on the conduct of non-aggressive cross-examination by experienced practitioners during cases, observed that the finest example he ever had in front of him was Sundaresh Menon, who never raised his voice, was always courteous, and proved utterly effective.

Today the Chartered Institute of Arbitrators has an international reputation that belies the size of the organization and often stretches the resources of the centre to the limit. In the long-term it must be in the interests of the Institute to establish strong regional offices in parts of the world like Singapore where membership is strong. Its unique global presence presents outstanding opportunities for members active in branches in their own countries, who can make a real difference to the development of arbitration. In Australia, for example, Institute members, with other organizations, have recently been granted amicus status in the high court for major arbitration appeals. The branches provide an invaluable network for continuing professional development, exchanging information and highlighting trends in dispute resolution. Margaret Rutherford reflected how 'a great feature of arbitration, at least for those of us in or associated with the

Lord Phillips of Worth Matravers.

Institute, has been the incredibly generous help which has always been readily available'. Each branch today is linked to a liaison trustee. Members worldwide are well served by the small and dedicated staff based in London. As one member, Mark Entwistle, notes, the strength of the Institute comes not only from the voluntary activities of so many members, but also from the service of its staff. 'I have found them to be unfailingly helpful, courteous and hard-working, and they deserve much more recognition from the membership'. Bennar Balkaya from Turkey, elected to the Board of Management in 2014, believes that relations between the branches and the centre have improved greatly, becoming much more transparent and responsive. The Institute today, she believes, has become a dynamic organization, its staff understanding very well the needs and concerns of members. Much of the credit for this must go to long-serving staff member Sue McLaughlin, latterly membership services manager, whose skills were recognized in her recent appointment as associate director with responsibility for education and training in Europe.

While serving in Iraq, Anthony Abrahams had been involved in resolving a dispute between Iraqi judges and a local army commander threatening to hinder the country's return to the rule of law. The experience made him a passionate advocate of the merits of ADR in helping the recovery of nations torn apart by war or internal conflict. This was a passion he shared with the first President he worked with, Jeffrey Elkinson, who also felt the Institute could do more to fulfil its charitable status. On taking office he had hoped that 'the Institute would go beyond its normal training locations and occasionally carry out training, perhaps on a pro bono basis, in places where it would have immediate benefits to the people who live there'. 'In such places,' he continued, 'one of the first institutions that stops working properly or at all is the court system. The need for alternative dispute resolution is critical as disputes need resolution to secure peace and harmony; [the Institute] can give the relevant training and those who are trained can pass on the training to others.' In 2013 this shared

117

vision led to a project in Sierra Leone. Following a visit to the Sierra Leonean High Commission in London, this was implemented by the Institute in association with a charity already working in the country with which another Institute Fellow, Richard Honey, was connected. The project was warmly welcomed by people in Sierra Leone, and the intention is to create a self-sustaining branch of the Institute there. At the end of September 2013 the Institute organized the first ADR training course to take place in the country in cooperation with the Sierra Leone Chamber of Commerce and the Sierra Leone General Legal Council. The courses were a huge success, fully subscribed and attended mainly by legal practitioners.

As one member, Mark Goodrich, noted in 2012, 'Arbitration will continue to grow. It is now the default choice for international contracts. It is a sensible career move, because the supply of work is never going to dry up'. This suggests that there is huge potential for the future growth of the Institute. As Jeffrey Elkinson remarked, 'we are the body that promotes arbitration principally through training'. For Thomas Halket, the qualifications offered by the Institute are 'the only meaningful credentials recognized around the world'. As well as arbitration, the Institute has a growing reputation in other forms of dispute resolution and its mediation accreditation, for instance, is regarded by some as the best in the world.

There are many attractions in arbitration as a second profession. It can be an immensely satisfying occupation. For Doug Jones, 'arbitration is definitely an art ... it's not about the application of standard procedures from one case to the next. Arbitration offers the flexibility of designing a process to suit a particular dispute.' Another member, Arthur Harverd, reflected that 'arbitration is never frustrating; the process is a fascinating one that always offers insights into different parts of the commercial world'. As it reaches its centenary, the Institute is a confident body, growing internationally, well respected as a learned society, well-established as an advocate for non-court dispute resolution in domestic jurisdictions worldwide, and poised to make advances in the field of international arbitration. And, as Jeffrey Elkinson said, 'it should be the most amazing force for good'.

Chartered
Institute of
Arbitrators

CIArb

DIPLOMA I

COMMERC

ma in International Commercial A

10 – 18 September 2011

Keble College, Oxford

INTERNATIONAL ARBITRATION

READING LIST – VOLUME 3

tration

61
62
63
64
65
66
67
36

81
82
83
84
85

27
28

87

LIST OF SUBSCRIBERS

ANTHONY ABRAHAMS MCIArb

MUHAMMAD KABIR ABUBAKAR ACIArb

DR O. T. ADEDEJI ACIArb

MAHMOOD AHMED MCIArb

UKPEME AKPAN MCIArb

MOHAMAD AL-DAH ACIArb

PENGIRAN ANAK PUTEH ALAM FCIArb

MOHAMED ALEM MCIArb

CHIEF JUSTICE JAMES ALLSOP

R. ANDREW FCIArb

MARY ANG'AWA FCIArb

BENNAR BALKAYA MCIArb

RENE M. BAPTISTE ACIArb

RICHARD BARNES MCIArb

ADNAN AMKHAN BAYNO FCIARB

ELOY E. BELLO IV ACIArb

LARS H. BERGQVIST ACIArb

WILLIAM MICHAEL BORDILL MCIArb

HON. CHARLES N. BROWER FCIArb C.Arb

CHARLES BROWN FCIArb

BERNARDO CARTONI MCIArb

SAMUEL CHACKO FCIArb C.Arb

MO Y. CHAN ACIArb Retired

JOHN COMRIE QC MCIArb

JUSTICE CLYDE CROFT FCIArb

KELPHENE CUNNINGHAM FCIArb

CHRIS DANCASTER FCIArb C.Arb

OLU DARAMOLA SAN FCIArb

FABRICE DAVIS MCIArb

ANDREW DAW ACIArb

MIRIAM DRIESSEN-REILLY FCIArb

HEW R. DUNDAS FCIArb C.Arb

JUSTICE DESMOND B. EDWARDS MCIArb

ABDULLAH SHERIF EL MAGHRABY MCIArb

ANTHONY D. J. GAFOOR FCIArb

ARTHUR E. GOLDSTRAW FCIArb C.Arb Retired

IVAN PAUL GRIXTI MCIArb

ROBERT HARTLE FCIArb

ARTHUR D. HARVERD FCIArb C.Arb

G. F. HAWKER FCIArb C.Arb

WAI TAK HEO MCIArb

CROWN ADVOCATE JASON HILL MCIArb

WILLIAM S. H. HUNG MCIArb

SIR CHRISTIAN OPUNABO INKO-TARIAH JP ACIArb

BERNIE IP ACIArb

JUSTICE (MRS) IFEOMA C. JOMBO-OFO ACIArb

DOUG JONES AO FCIArb C.Arb

KAISI KALAMBO MCIArb

NEIL KAPLAN CBE QC FCIArb C.Arb

WAJ KHAN ACIArb

KETHI KILONZO FCIArb

MUTULA C. KILONZO Jr ACIArb

M. A. R. KNIGHT MCIArb

EDMUND J. KRONENBURG FCIArb

GRAHAME LAIRD FCIArb

JOHN LANGLOIS OBE FCIArb C.Arb

STANLEY W. H. LAU MCIArb

YOANN LE BIHAN ACIArb

THIERRY LINARES FCIArb

CLIFFORD LINCOLN FCIArb

VICTORIA LIOUTA MCIArb

SIMON J. LOWE FCIArb

GEORGE MATHIESON FCIArb C.Arb

DR PETER MAYNARD ACIArb

DAVID MCCASKILL FCIArb

SUE MCLAUGHLIN MCIArb

CHIEF JUSTICE SUNDARESH MENON

PETER L. MICHAELSON FCIArb C.Arb

WENDY MILES FCIArb

J. A. MONSON ACIArb

ROBERT MORGAN FCIArb

RICHARD H. MORRIS FCIArb

WILLIAM MWEEMBA MCIArb

DANNY NG

JIMMY NUI ACIArb

M. R. NUNNS FCIArb Retired

TIMUCIN DENIZ OGRETIR FCIArb

WAHID ENITAN OSHODI MCIArb

NICHOLAS PADFIELD QC FCIArb

MICHAEL PEER FCIArb

MAURICE PLEASANCE FCIArb Retired

ALMON CHIN HUNG POON MCIArb

IAN PRUDDEN ACIArb

ANTHONY M. RAMAN-NAIKAN ACIArb

SHAHEEL KUMAR JOY RAMPHUL FCIArb

DENNIS N. RAMPLEY MCIArb Retired

JOHN RAWSTRON ACIArb

JOHN REDMOND FCIArb C.Arb

PETER REES QC FCIArb C.Arb

ALAN JOHN ROBINSON ACIArb Retired

THIAGO RODOVALHO ACIArb

DEREK ROEBUCK MCIArb

GAUDENZIO ROSSI MCIArb

JOHN RUNDELL FCIArb

PROFESSOR J. R. SALTER ACIArb Retired

FREDERIC Z. SAMELIAN MCIArb

FABIANO SANNINO ACIArb

WILLIAM SAUNDERS ACIArb

DIANA J. SAWE TANUI MCIArb

WILM SCHARLEMANN FCIArb

JEFFERY SEWELL MCIArb

VICTORIA ANNE SEWELL MCIArb

AUDLEY SHEPPARD FCIArb

MICHAEL STEPHENS FCIArb

NEVILLE TAIT FCIArb C.Arb

BRIAN TAM ACIArb

ADRIAS TAN FCIArb

JAMES TAYLOR FCIArb

NEIL B. TAYLOR FCIArb

NIMBLE THOMPSON MCIArb Retired

CHRISTOPHER TO FCIArb C.Arb

THOMAS SO SHIN TSUNG

W. RAY TURNER FCIArb Retired

ANITA UDOH ACIARB

B. W. VIGRASS OBE FCIArb Retired

JOHN EZRA VILLEGAS MCIArb

KATIA VOLODINE

MARKUS H. WANGER FCIArb

JILL WARD MCIArb

MATTHEW J. WILLS FCIArb

KWOK-CHEUNG WONG MCIArb

AMOS POM HIN WU MCIArb

INDEX

Picture Credits

All of the images within the book belong to the Chartered Institute of Arbitrators, unless noted below. Every effort has been made to contact the copyright owners of images featured in this book. In the case of an inadvertent omission, please contact the TMI Group at the address on the rear jacket flap.

34 © The Art Archive/Alamy; 42 Hulton Archive/Getty Images; 41 (L) Library of Congress; 37 (L) London Metropolitan Archives, City of London; 32 Mary Evans/Everett Collection; 43, 64 Mary Evans Picture Library; 35 (R), 41 (R), 61, 65, 91 © National Portrait Gallery, London; 62 Royal Photographic Society/National Media Museum/ Science & Society Picture Library; 66 UN Photo/Marvin Bolotsky.